will benefit all of us. If it's true that a person's way of life is determined by his view of God, you should expect life to be better after reading this book. Chip, as usual, has hit the nail on the head."

Randy Pope, pastor,
Perimeter Church, Atlanta, Georgia

"A fresh look at the beauty of who God is will never leave us unchanged. We are made in the image of our Creator, and to live out the beauty of his person in our lives will never leave others unchanged. Chip Ingram has given us a gift here of a greater focus on what that beauty actually entails."

Darryl DelHousaye, president,
Phoenix Seminary, Phoenix, Arizona

"One of my favorite passages of Scripture is Isaiah 55:8: '"For My thoughts are not your thoughts, nor are your ways My ways," declares the LORD.' As I read Chip's new book, I kept thinking of those words. So grounded in Scripture. So focused on Jesus. Chip helps us see God's thoughts. He helps us know God as he wants to be known."

Bryant Wright, senior pastor,
Johnston Ferry Baptist Church, Marietta, Georgia

"The crying need today is not for people to know more about God, or even to 'enjoy' an experience with God, but to be shaken by the reality of who God is, to have their faith turned right side up by the nearness of eternity. *The Real God: How He Longs for You to See Him* will kindle afresh your passion to know, firsthand, the God of the universe."

James MacDonald, pastor,
Harvest Bible Chapel, Rolling Meadows, Illinois

"Like Chip, as a young man I was fascinated by A. W. Tozer's *The Knowledge of the Holy*. It's great to see a book that leads today's generation into a similar contemplation of the mysteries of God—without abandoning the anchor of solid biblical theology.

"Stressed out by life's instability? Chip reminds you of the rock solid foundation on which you can always rely: the unchanging attributes of God. Tired of the channel-changing, short attention span, shallow thinking of today's culture? Chip helps you focus on the deepest possible object of meditation in the universe—the nature of God himself—in a way that's accessible and intriguing. This is the rare book that is simple without being shallow; that helps calm you while also challenging you.

"I believe most of the problems and stresses we bring on ourselves are a result of poor theology, particularly about the nature of God. After being reminded by Chip of God's sovereignty, holiness, love, faithfulness, and more, my own joy and serenity were renewed! I needed this book."

Rene Schlaepfer, senior pastor,
Twin Lakes Church, Aptos, California

THE
REAL
GOD

Other books by Chip Ingram

Good to Great in God's Eyes

Love, Sex, and Lasting Relationships

Finding God When You Need Him Most

Overcoming Emotions that Destroy (with Becca Johnson)

Sex180: The Next Revolution (with Tim Walker)

Culture Shock

The Invisible War

The Real Heaven

THE
REAL
GOD

How He Longs for You to See Him

CHIP INGRAM

BakerBooks

a division of Baker Publishing Group
Grand Rapids, Michigan

Published by Baker Books
a division of Baker Publishing Group
P.O. Box 6287, Grand Rapids, MI 49516-6287
www.bakerbooks.com

Previously published under the title *God: As He Longs for You to See Him*

Printed in the United States of America

Library of Congress Cataloging-in-Publication Data
Names: Ingram, Chip, 1954– author.
Title: The real God : how He longs for you to see Him / Chip Ingram.
Other titles: God, as He longs for you to see Him
Description: Grand Rapids, MI : Baker Books, 2016. | "Previously published under the title: God, as He longs for you to see Him." | Includes bibliographical references.
Identifiers: LCCN 2016022009 | ISBN 9780801018893 (pbk.)
Subjects: LCSH: God (Christianity)—Attributes.
Classification: LCC BT130 .I54 2016 | DDC 231/.4—dc23
LC record available at https://lccn.loc.gov/2016022009

Published in association with Yates & Yates, www.yates2.com

19 20 21 22   7 6 5

I dedicate this book to all who earnestly seek to know God as he is and long to reflect his likeness in every moment of every day in every way.

CONTENTS

ACKNOWLEDGMENTS

I wish to thank Neil Wilson and Chris Tiegreen for their insightful help with this book, and Vicki Crumpton for her excellent editing, encouragement, and overall management of the project. I am eternally grateful for the missionary in Asia who introduced me to the study of God's attributes, the honest feedback of friends and family, and most of all for the sustaining grace and endurance given by my SOVEREIGN GOD AND KING to finish the task assigned to me. What a privilege!

INTRODUCTION

I was twenty-one years old at the time. It was my first visit to Asia, traveling as part of an evangelistic basketball team. While in Hong Kong, we stayed in the home of a veteran missionary who captivated my interest. On one particular morning, he invited my fellow players and me into his study for a discussion.

Although the entire room we entered was lined with books, one wall of shelves filled with paperbacks immediately caught my attention. As he walked over to that particular bookcase, the missionary explained that he had a well-established habit of reading one Christian paperback every day. He had learned speed-reading techniques to go with his obvious God-given quick mind. I could tell from the titles that he wasn't just engaged in light reading, since I recognized many of the classics on those tightly packed shelves.

He and I had already had several conversations, and I think he spotted a spiritual hunger in me that drew him to me. I realized later that I was the primary target of that gathering, for which I owe him an eternal debt of gratitude. He selected a volume from one of the shelves and turned to face us, looking directly at me.

The warmth in his eyes told me I needed to pay attention to what he was about to say. My teammates were busy finding seats, so I wasn't surprised when he said, "Chip, have you ever read this book?" He held it out to me invitingly.

I took the book and looked at the cover. Not only hadn't I read it, but I had to admit I'd never even heard of it. He accepted my admission with a smile and then said, "It's the best book I've ever read." I looked down at it again, determined to remember the title and author so I could read it when I got back to the States. But he wasn't finished. "Why don't you take it and read it during your stay here in Hong Kong. You can return it before you leave."

I can't describe the specific reasons, but the character of this missionary challenged me deeply. I wanted to learn what he had learned and read what he had read. Little did I know that the book he had just placed in my hands would change the entire course of my life.

Later that day I opened the slim volume and began a journey that I have continued ever since. Before I left Hong Kong, my missionary friend allowed me to keep as a gift what had become my constant companion during those days. In fact, that same book is still a regular occupant of my briefcase everywhere I go.

A single sentence, early in the book, had a powerful impact on my life. The author opened by saying,

> What comes to our minds when we think about God is the most important thing about us.[1]

The book was on the attributes of God, and the author introduced me to ways of seeing the God of the Bible that I had never thought about, let alone imagined. Almost immediately, my prayers began to change as I realized how big, powerful, and all-knowing the God I was praying to really is. Identity issues and struggles with guilt began to dissipate as I pondered the depths of God's forgiveness and compassion. My awareness of God's majesty and holiness came into sharper focus even as I realized, as never before, that the God of creation was eager to be friends with me.

This book is an invitation to you to join my journey. For some of you, the content of these pages will be very familiar. Those of you who have been exposed to A. W. Tozer and J. I. Packer and others like them will quickly realize how indebted I am to them. I have tried to carefully credit their (and others') exact words when I have used them, but those who know the classic writers on the character of God will hear the echoes of their influence on every page. I neither claim nor aim to be in their category as scholars. My life has been immeasurably enriched by the many who have faithfully used their thinking and writing gifts to inform my own voice.

Readers with theological experience will notice the limited scope of this book. When it comes to the character of God, any book will reach its limits long before it exhausts its topic. This book is not intended to be exhaustive, but instead to be inspirational and practical. My aim is to engage the reader in a lifelong pursuit of knowing, seeing, and experiencing the Real God.

No spiritual exercise in my life has had greater impact on me than my continual reviewing, meditating on, and applying the implications of God's traits in my daily living. I have been repeatedly stopped, stirred, or strengthened by being brought back to who God really is instead of who I might casually conceive him to be. Once you begin this journey, you will discover God has something new to show you about himself every day.

My hope and my prayer is that as you read this book, God will do for you what he's been doing in me since I began my study of him—expanding your mind and enlarging your heart as you begin to see God as he longs to be seen.

1

IT'S ALL IN HOW YOU SEE IT

In the middle of my sophomore year, a student named Denise transferred to our school from another college. I had been a Christian for about three years. I was growing spiritually, and I wanted to be as faithful as possible with each opportunity to learn or serve. As an eager, motivated believer, I had begun stepping into leadership roles in campus ministry. Denise immediately jumped into campus ministry events. Within about thirty seconds of meeting her, I began to feel an overwhelming sense of intimidation. Both her credentials and her actions thoroughly impressed me.

For some reason, I felt very self-conscious around her. She was so "together" that I was sure she would instantly notice my insecurities and struggles. What if I made the wrong impression? I wanted so much for her to like me that I quit being myself and froze up. I didn't want to make a fool of myself. I nervously focused on making sure I didn't say something stupid that would come across as spiritual ignorance. The result, of course, was that I didn't say much at all. It wasn't a very promising beginning for a friendship.

In the months that followed, I watched Denise blossom with grace and humility as she got to know the other people at school. She seemed to lead with effortless skill. She was a natural to head up the women's Bible studies, and her advice was always sought for various ministry decisions on campus.

All the while, I longed for her to know the real me so we could be friends. We were like-minded on so many things. And my respect for her was in the stratosphere. But once I started down this awkward path of insecurity, it quickly got more and more difficult to unveil my true self. The longer it went on, the more intimidated I became. Whenever I was around her, I was paralyzed. If I saw her in a Bible study, at a team meeting, or just around campus, I would always struggle to have anything to say that got beyond superficial chatting and politeness. And when I did manage to speak, I was usually so tense that it came out sounding stupid. Instead of getting closer and closer, she seemed farther and farther away. I was sure her impression of me just kept getting worse. I was convinced that everything I did confirmed to her that I was a spiritual dud.

For two years, I carried on a superficial relationship with this girl I held in such high regard. Externally, others noticed nothing. We were both part of the leadership team on campus and the ministry was going well. Inside, I always felt like a puppy swimming. The guy others could see looked calm enough, but beneath the surface I was scrambling to stay afloat. I was just glad Denise was such a mature Christian; if she weren't, she would certainly be laughing about me behind my back with her friends.

The Veil Is Lifted

Finally one evening during our senior year, Denise needed a ride down to Wheeling, a town about thirty minutes away from campus. She asked me in her typically gracious manner, "Is there any way you can give me a ride?"

"Sure," I said without thinking. I was usually happy to offer anyone a ride, let alone a beautiful, godly coed.

But the minute we climbed into my little green Volkswagen Beetle, I began to feel uncomfortable again. With miles of twisting, turning road ahead of us, there was no escape. It was worse than a blind date. My Beetle never felt smaller.

For the first ten minutes, there was awkward silence. As my sweaty palms gripped the steering wheel, I desperately searched for a coherent sentence to utter. Denise was probably struggling to think of some common ground that she could share with the mute simpleton riding beside her. She had to be regretting her choice of chauffeur.

Eventually, she broke the ice. "Chip," she began, "could I share something with you?"

"Go ahead." I was relieved she took the lead.

"There's something that I think has been a barrier in our relationship for the last two years," she began.

Uh-oh, I thought, *now she's finally going to tell me what she thinks of me.*

"You know," she continued, "I've watched God grow you these last two years. You've really stepped up to the plate in the men's ministry. And well, I don't know if this has ever happened to you, but here's the thing. From the first time I met you, I've just been so intimidated by you."

My jaw hit the floor.

"And I'm afraid I've been so uncomfortable around you that I've never felt like I could just be myself. Now that we're finishing our senior year, I feel kind of sad about that. But I just wanted to get that out in the open."

If we hadn't been on a straightaway, I might have run right off the road. Stunned at first, I finally burst out laughing. "You mean *you* were intimidated by *me*?!" I howled. "*I* was the one intimidated by *you*! Every time I'd try to say something, the words came out all wrong." We both had a good laugh, and from that day forward, Denise and I became good friends.

I'll never forget how my assumptions and misconceptions about Denise were a barrier in our relationship. Our inaccurate views of each other stunted the growth of our friendship. The friendship and encouragement we could have shared during those two years were put on hold—all because I had a warped perception of her, and she had a warped perception of me.

A Clearer Picture

The lesson I learned with Denise has divine application. What you think about God shapes your whole relationship with him. In addition, what you believe *God* thinks about *you* determines how close you will grow toward him. Many of us have formed a picture of God from impressions we've picked up throughout our life. Consciously, or unconsciously, our families, teachers, friends, and churches have impacted our picture of God. Our culture consistently sends us messages about how to see God as well. All of us have been affected and can carry a distorted image of God. If we see him as an impulsive policeman, we'll always be walking on eggshells. If we see him as a vengeful judge, we'll always feel guilty. If we see him as an apathetic father, we will struggle with believing he loves us. If we think he's just like us, we'll be casual about our sin. But are those ideas accurate? What if they're not true at all? Misperceptions about God can certainly create a barrier in your relationship with him. And meanwhile, the friendship, love, and encouragement you could be sharing with your heavenly Father are never realized—all because of wrong assumptions about him.

What you think about God shapes your whole relationship with him.

In addition, what you believe God thinks about you determines how close you will grow toward him.

This dynamic is also true about every relationship in your life. Our relationships are formed by our perceptions of each other. How you see somebody makes all the difference in the world, as does how you think the other person sees you. Our perceptions then affect how we act toward each other. I thought Denise didn't like me. I thought I didn't measure up. And it didn't make a bit of difference that she actually thought very highly of me, because I assumed she didn't. My mind was made up. Because she didn't like me, I did not try to get to know her. I was operating under my perception of Denise and what I thought she thought rather than the truth.

So, let me ask you life's most important questions:

- What do you think about God?

- What do you think he thinks about you?

- How do these perceptions affect your relationship with him?

Think about that. He created you for closeness, love, and friendship. Are you experiencing that? His Word is meant to disclose his deep, personal thoughts to you, and prayer is meant for you to disclose your deep, personal thoughts to him. Are you enjoying that kind of intimacy? Do you feel like you can never do anything right, that God is "down on you" or waiting for you to mess up so he can discipline you? Do you often find it hard to pray? Does the thought that you are the object of his utter delight seem foreign to you? Are you living much of your life in fear? Do you secretly struggle with obeying him because you think you might miss out on the fun in life if you are completely committed to him? Your answers to these questions will tell you a lot about your perceptions of God.

A Longing for God

If there's one thing I've learned about people, it's the fact that we all long for the fulfillment that comes from a close, intimate relationship with God. Some may have become deluded by false philosophies, blocked him out of their lives, or simply become distracted by other things. But underneath it all, God has created each of us with an innate desire for deep, meaningful fellowship with him.

Think about that desire for just a minute. Try to listen to it. Is it speaking to you right now? Can you hear its voice crying out? You may be used to thinking that God is a distant, impersonal observer who is too busy to be concerned with you. Despite your desire, he may have always seemed out of reach. Forget that for a moment. Just for now, can you set aside the feelings that tell you you're not good enough to be accepted by him, or that he's been unfair, or he doesn't care? That may be extremely difficult if those feelings are deeply ingrained, but ask God to help you, and then do your best to let go of them.

Now imagine breaking through all those misperceptions and somehow experiencing complete acceptance and deep intimacy with your heavenly Father . . . the God of the universe . . . the One who created you and delights in you. What if all the hurts that you've felt from other people could be dissolved in his perfect love? What if your disappointments could be instantly reversed by the complete satisfaction he brings? What if you could stop looking at God through all the distortions of life and begin to look at life through him instead? Can you picture yourself in a perfect relationship with God like that?

Believe it or not, that desire lives deep inside you right now. You may not feel it very strongly at this moment, but it's there. Perhaps it's a faint memory, but the longing remains. You may have learned to divert that desire to other things over the years, but you cannot squelch it completely. It is the key to finding purpose in a life that can seem overwhelming on some days and absolutely meaningless on others.

In the pages that follow, I hope you will begin to feel that desire rekindled and fanned into a flame, perhaps for the first time. If you're like many people, including me, your misconceptions about God have formed a barrier that keeps you from experiencing him as he really is—and as he wants to be seen.

Deep inside, I felt like Denise and I were meant to be great friends. Our hearts beat in rhythm on so many things. Her life represented the kind of person I wanted to become. There was so much to be gained if we could just make a connection . . . so much to enjoy if only I could have set aside my misperceptions of her. An authentic, deep friendship was waiting just beyond our common misunderstanding. The same is true about our understanding of God, but there's so much more at stake.

Yet Another Moment of Truth

Several years ago, I learned another unforgettable lesson in the way my misconceptions about God keep me from the benefits of truly knowing him. Our church in Santa Cruz, California, was experiencing tremendous expansion. As with any growing organization, there were growing pains. The response to God's Word was overflowing our seating capacity. Our resources were stretched to their breaking point. The pressure to provide solutions was overwhelming. I felt neck-deep in capital campaign meetings, day-to-day church management, and preparing messages for the ever-expanding crowds on weekends. The weekdays were a blur of activity. To be honest, I struggled with depression as I felt the increasing demands and pressures of the church's growth. I appeared publicly to be enthusiastic and successful, but inwardly I experienced many moments of despair.

If that wasn't enough, our construction plans were delayed by city ordinances and financial challenges. It seemed like so much was going wrong behind the scenes—little glitches and huge obstacles. Most people were unaware of the extent of the problems, but I couldn't help thinking that God would have taken care of all these heavy matters if only I had done something better. I believed that the entire weight of the church's ministry rested on my shoulders. I falsely assumed that the problems were the result of mistakes I had made or of inadequacies in my leadership.

I "knew" much of what you are about to read in this book. I believed and understood certain clear ideas about God. I had even experienced the spiritual effect of these principles in my life. But, there's a difference between understanding God's attributes intellectually and letting them affect the way you live your life. The truth needed to sink in. Like all of us, I was a "work in progress," and God was (and is) far from finished with me. I still had certain misconceptions about him that needed to be clarified. The circumstances I was in, just like the circumstances you are in, were simply another opportunity for God to teach me something deeper about himself. That seems so obvious now, but being in that situation had me demoralized, tentative, doubtful, and exhausted.

One day, it all came to a head. I sat alone in my office with an overwhelming sense that everything was depending on me. I was exhausted and discouraged, and I honestly wondered if I could continue. While crying out to God for some relief, I glanced down and noticed a gift that had been anonymously placed on my desk by a church member—a frame containing the text from Zephaniah 3:17, a somewhat obscure Old Testament verse. Through tears, I read the words and felt the voice of God speaking directly to me.

> The LORD your God is with you,
>   he is mighty to save.
> He will take great delight in you,
>   he will quiet you with his love,
>   he will rejoice over you with singing.

It suddenly seemed as though God were right there in the room with me. I sensed his power, and it convinced me that he could bring complete resolution to the things that were pressing down on me. Best of all, I could feel his absolute pleasure and delight in me—regardless of how I performed in that situation. He reached right past my inadequate offering and my insecure efforts and embraced me. I could picture him rejoicing and singing over me like a mother who can't believe she gets to be the mother. Somehow, as that awareness of God's delight filled me, the work I was doing or the obstacles I was facing didn't seem all that important after all. As God lifted the weight off my shoulders, I shamelessly smiled as I realized I wasn't supposed to try to carry it in the first place.

Looking back, I now realize that my pre-Christian ideas about God were still very much with me. I had seen God as someone who dispensed rewards to those who were good and crushing discipline for those who were bad. When things were not going well, I assumed I had done something wrong. My misperceptions of God had produced a very driven person who struggled with being a workaholic for the first decade of his ministry. Rooted deeply in any driven achiever is the sense that who you are is determined by what you do. As this verse washed over my heart and soul, God's Spirit used the words to recalibrate my view of him—to separate my performance from my identity. Like a lightbulb coming on inside my head, I made the connection that God's love and delight had absolutely nothing to do with my work or my performance.

I began a new era in my relationship with Christ. In that instant, I realized in a fresh way that God is on my side . . . that he really delights in me. For the first time in a long while, I was able to separate my performance from what God thought of me. I was free to do what I could and to simply trust him for the rest. And it all started with that subtle change in my perception of God. His Word removed some spiritual filters that had obstructed my view of him.

In the weeks and months that followed, I plunged myself deep into this new picture of God. I explored passage after passage in Scripture describing a heavenly Father who not only loves me, but cares deeply about every little nuance of my life. With great concern, he watches over all my comings and goings. He may not always intervene the way I want him to, but he's always present and involved.

A strange thing happened as a result of that experience. The more I learned the truth about God, the more I felt our relationship strengthen.

And it was all because I was uncovering my misperceptions and discovering who he really is. I saw glimpses of God's character so satisfying that they have kept me coming back for more. I also discovered how easy it is to slip into the old misperceptions. They are deeply entrenched in our thought patterns. We may get out of those holes with God's help, but if we don't watch where we step, we can easily fall back in. When that happens, it's usually because we've forgotten something about God's character—or we discover we haven't learned it yet.

My friendship with Denise began to flourish when we discovered the truth about each other. What would it be like if you applied that same dynamic to your relationship with God? Deep inside, you already long to know him intimately. Can you imagine a God who knows you intimately and loves you beyond what you can comprehend? Can you imagine the transforming impact that would have on your life?

A Change of Perception

In the chapters of this book, I want to help you develop an image of God as he longs to be seen. He has taken several millennia, inspired hundreds of pages of Scripture, and gone through a traumatic incarnation to paint an accurate portrait of himself. He obviously cares what we think about him. He wants us to see him clearly, attribute by amazing attribute.

Along the way, we will dismantle the common misconceptions about God that keep us from getting as close as he longs for us to be. You will have numerous opportunities to identify your own misconceptions and exchange them for the view God has given us of himself. But I want to go beyond what you can know about God's qualities to offer you tools you can use to implement those attributes in your daily life. It's one thing for us to reach a rational conclusion that God is good. It's entirely different to let that truth begin to affect the way we make decisions, invest in relationships, interpret events, and look to the future. Every one of God's attributes has that potential. I had the thrill of seeing God change me—heart, soul, and mind—as I gradually applied the truth of who he is to the way I live. If you will join me on this journey, I promise to share with you the lessons I've learned, the mistakes I've made, and the helps I've discovered in my walk with God. This is the beginning of an exciting adventure!

It's time to delete the photo effects that have distorted our picture of God. Let him unveil an amazing portrait of himself. Seeing God as he longs to be seen will change you forever.

2

SEEING GOD WITH 20/20 VISION

was frustrated, but I wasn't quite sure why. I had taught God's Word for over twenty years on college campuses, at schools, and in local churches, and I had never had this problem before. My mind simply wasn't "clicking."

In the past, my thoughts flowed effortlessly. I could connect the truth of God's Word with the audience to whom I was speaking. But something had changed. The thoughts weren't coming. I often had to stop and reread my notes silently to get back into the flow of the message. My "pregnant pauses" weren't meant so much to give my listeners time to think and reflect on what I had just said; they were to give me time to look at my notes and make my next point.

That may not seem like a big deal to many people, but for those who preach, this was like flying an airplane without instruments. Had I lost my gift? Was there some sin in my life? Was I in the first stages of some debilitating mental disease? I secretly pondered these and even less logical possibilities.

Months later, while preaching on a very technical passage, I was quoting a very old commentary that was written with very small print. I took my reading glasses to the pulpit with me so I could read from the old book. After reading the selection, I unconsciously glanced down at my notes. Eureka! I realized that my problem was simple. I had not been seeing my own notes clearly. I had no idea how distorted they were until I saw them clearly with my reading glasses. Though I wasn't off by much, I wasn't seeing with 20/20 vision. The energy required to focus and refocus my eyes was causing my brain to freeze. It was busy trying to see rather than to think.

What's really puzzling is that I was totally unaware of it. My vision became distorted so gradually that it was imperceptible. Bad vision was negatively impacting my calling from God, and it sent me down paths of fear and anxiety that are embarrassing to admit.

This is exactly what happens to all of us in our perception of God. When we don't see him with 20/20 vision, it distorts every other area of our lives. So I invite you now on a sacred and holy journey, one that must be taken with great care and sobriety. And one that must begin with a warning.

Be advised. You are entering holy ground. You are welcome to tread here, but do so attentively. The study of God himself is the loftiest and most significant pursuit that you could ever undertake. The rewards are great, but the risks are real. You are not going where no one has gone before; you're going somewhere far better—to a place you were ultimately designed to explore.

Left to ourselves, we human beings regularly stumble into three gaping errors as we are learning to think accurately about God:

- We tend to assume that God is just like us.

- We tend to reduce him to measurable and controllable terms.

- We tend to overlook the obvious and significant ways that he has revealed himself to us.

As we move into these holy moments and meet the character of God, I trust that the following words of A. W. Tozer will continually ring in our ears.

> What comes into our minds when we think about God is the most important thing about us.

> The history of mankind will probably show that no people has ever risen above its religion, and man's spiritual history will positively demonstrate that no religion has ever been greater than its idea of God.[1]

Please reread that statement, slowly. This is serious business. Nothing in all your life will impact your relationship with God, your relationship with people, your self-view, your decisions, and your purpose like the way you think of God. Everything in your life consciously or unconsciously comes back to one thing: Whom do you visualize God to be in your heart? And where did you get that picture? Who we are and what we become cannot be separated from our understanding of God. Tozer continues,

> Worship is pure or base as the worshiper entertains high or low thoughts of God. For this reason the gravest question before the Church is always God Himself, and the most portentous fact about any man is not what he at any given time may say or do, but what he in his deep heart conceives God to be like.[2]

What if he's right? What if the most important thing about your life, your future, your relationships, and all that you are is whether you have a clear, accurate picture of God?

Tozer is only getting started. He continues with a fascinating application that I believe is absolutely true. He writes, "We tend by a secret law of the soul to move toward our mental image of God."[3] He applies this principle to both individual Christians and the church at large. The way we act as believers and as a church states clearly what we actually think about God.

> **"We tend by a secret law of the soul to move toward our mental image of God."**
>
> **—A. W. Tozer**

If Tozer is right, then we need to see God with 20/20 vision. As much as it is humanly possible, we must get an accurate, clear picture of who the Creator of the universe is and exactly what he is like. We want to encounter, embrace, and know God as he is. And here's the motivation: until you know God as he is, you'll never become all that he's created you to be.

Vision Exam

From time to time you and I need to have our spiritual eyes examined so that they can refocus and gain a wider, clearer perspective on God as he has made himself known to us. Scripture can be truth enlightening our souls, helping us realize God is so much bigger, so much more holy, so much more loving, so much wiser than we can fully grasp.

One of the first things optometrists do when they want to examine your eyes is to "challenge" them with alternative lenses. They use a device that radically alters your vision by changing focal lengths. I'm about to "challenge" your spiritual eyes with three lenses of biblical revelation. Each of these lenses represents a fact about God that we cannot avoid or ignore if we want to have 20/20 vision when it comes to him. These may or may not seem obvious to you, but the way they are clarified in Scripture makes them an essential part of a right understanding of God. The verses you are about to read might overwhelm you. Read them slowly and thoughtfully, asking God to open the eyes of your heart as well as your mind. These three focal lenses will help get your spiritual vision re-clarified as we prepare to see God as he longs for you to see him.

> **Until you know God as he is, you'll never become all that he's created you to be.**

First Focal Lens: God is not like us!

It seems so obvious, doesn't it? God is not like us. When we honestly look at him, we won't see a reflection of ourselves. The Bible tells us we are made in his image and there are similarities, but God is not like us. He is not a bigger or better version of human beings; we are simply intended to be a startling and amazing likeness of him. At our best, we only represent a hint of who he is.

The Scriptures state God's otherness with overwhelming clarity. Let's begin with Isaiah:

> "To whom will you compare me?
> Or who is my equal?" says the Holy One.
> Lift your eyes and look to the heavens:
> Who created all these?
> He who brings out the starry host one by one,
> and calls them each by name.

> Because of his great power and mighty strength,
>> not one of them is missing.
>
> Why do you say, O Jacob,
>> and complain, O Israel,
> "My way is hidden from the LORD;
>> my cause is disregarded by my God"?
> Do you not know?
>> Have you not heard?
> The LORD is the everlasting God,
>> the Creator of the ends of the earth.
> He will not grow tired or weary,
>> and his understanding no one can fathom. (Isa. 40:25–28)

God is not like us. People get tired and weary; God does not. There are things we don't understand; God never even has a question come to his mind. He is all-powerful, he is all-knowing, he is all-wise. All the best in us is a faint impression of what he is. He's not like us.

David, a man after God's own heart, made this confession: "How great you are, O Sovereign LORD! There is no one like you, and there is no God but you, as we have heard with our own ears" (2 Sam. 7:22). Another psalmist writes, "Be still, and know that I am God" (Ps. 46:10). Until we're ready to be still, we will not be ready to know God.

The apostle Paul, no stranger to humbling encounters with God, pushed the limits of language when he tried to compose an appropriate doxology for God. He had just penned some of the most profound insights on the free will of man, the sovereignty of God, and the complexity of life. Then he takes a deep breath and writes,

> Oh, the depth of the riches of the wisdom and knowledge of
>> God!
> How unsearchable his judgments,
>> and his paths beyond tracing out!

Who has known the mind of the Lord?
    Or who has been his counselor?
Who has ever given to God,
    that God should repay him?
For from him and through him and to him are all things.
    To him be the glory forever! Amen. (Rom. 11:33–36)

The answer to these rhetorical questions is obvious—no one. No one has known God's mind; no one has been his counselor; and God owes no one. Notice the last phrase, "From him"—God is the source of everything. "Through him"—he is the instrumental cause of all that exists. And ultimately it's "to him"—for his glory. He is not like you or me. He's not like any created being.

Second Focal Lens: Left to ourselves, we tend to reduce God to manageable terms.

In other words we shrink him. Faced with this awesome, all-knowing, all-powerful, holy God, the exposure makes us so uncomfortable that we turn on our mental compactors and shrink him. We look for a little God-box, or we try to tame him, or we seek to manage him. Since we can't do this with the true God, we invent a new deity who will submit to our wishes.

THE SHRINKING GOD SYNDROME

Instead of falling down as servants before this awesome God, we try to get him to be our servant so we can use him for our purposes. Follow the progression as Paul describes the way people respond to the invisible, immortal, awesome God:

For although they knew God, they neither glorified him as God nor gave thanks to him, but their thinking became futile and their foolish hearts were darkened. Although they claimed to be wise, they became fools and exchanged the glory of the immortal God for images made to look like mortal man and birds and animals and reptiles. (Rom. 1:21–23)

He begins with the universal acknowledgment of God's existence from which people deliberately turn away in their thinking. Their reasoning leads to the reductionism that exchanges God for things. They turned away from their Creator so they could pretend to create.

The process Paul traced continues today. Left to ourselves we reduce God to manageable terms. We treat him lightly. We make him accountable to us rather than humbly realizing we are completely accountable to him. Our consumer culture often sees God as a cosmic vending machine that we can visit when we are in need. We are interested in what God can deliver at the push of a button. This was the lesson God taught Job in a remarkable way (Job 38–41). For thirty-seven chapters, Job and his friends discussed their views of God. They each created a framework and expected God to conform to their design. Finally in chapter 38, the Lord spoke. He didn't excuse or explain himself. Instead he simply confronted Job and company with an avalanche of questions. How could they begin to discuss God's purposes when they couldn't demonstrate a little understanding of the blueprints of creation? God will not be managed.

When it comes to examples of human reductionism, perhaps our least finest moment is recorded in Exodus 32:1–6, a classic passage that describes the behavior of people who experienced some of the most remarkable demonstrations of God's power in history. They saw a proud nation devastated and humiliated in order to gain their freedom. They walked between walls of water, parted exclusively for their passage. God offered them his visible presence in a pillar of cloud by day and fire by night.

Moses is on the mountain receiving the Ten Commandments. As you read this passage, note how uncertainty, fear, and an inability to control the situation affected this group of people. Although they had seen the power of the invisible God in miracles, they reduced him into something that they could see and manage.

"When the people saw that Moses was so long in coming down from the mountain, they gathered around Aaron and said, 'Come, make us gods who will go before us. As for this fellow Moses who brought us up out of Egypt, we don't know what has happened to him'" (Exod. 32:1). They concluded Moses was AWOL. Since they couldn't see either Moses or his God, they decided some manufactured "gods" would do just as well.

Given a wonderful opportunity to lead, Aaron chose instead to follow the crowd. "Aaron answered them, 'Take off the gold earrings that your wives, your sons and your daughters are wearing, and bring them to me.' So all the people took off their earrings and brought them to Aaron. He took what they handed him and made it into an idol cast in the shape of a calf, fashioning it with a tool. Then they said, 'These are your gods, O Israel, who brought you up out of Egypt'" (vv. 2–4). They reduced God to a calf made out of recycled jewelry and then proceeded to rewrite history. They gave credit to the previously nonexistent calf for being the god who led them out of captivity.

What on earth was Aaron thinking? Moses had left him in charge. Perhaps Aaron thought he could keep things from getting out of hand by reminding the people that there was still a "Lord" in the picture. "When Aaron saw this, he built an altar in front of the calf and announced, 'Tomorrow there will be a festival to the LORD'" (v. 5). Like us, Aaron forgot God doesn't share the spotlight with anyone. "So the next day the people rose early and sacrificed burnt offerings and presented fellowship offerings. Afterward they sat down to eat and drink and got up to indulge in revelry" (v. 6). This was not the revelry of a joyful worship service. The word implies base sensuality, a casting off of restraints. This party was a "what happens in Vegas, stays in Vegas" kind of party.

And did you notice what happened? Does their line of thinking seem familiar? "We can't see this God and so we're going to make something up and then we're going to call it god. We're going to worship it, create a religion to go with it, burn offerings to it, and then experiment with any behaviors that strike our fancy—but we'll call them all religious exercises."

What seems like obvious foolishness viewed backward in time is a little harder to spot when we're actually doing the same thing today. You may be saying to yourself, "I don't make idols! I mean, I can't remember the last time I went home and said, 'Excuse me, honey, I'm going to the family room to pray to our cow bust wall hanging. I think it might do some good.'"

No, that's not what we do. But we do create our own idols. They may take the form of food, image, wealth, work, family, friends . . . the list is endless. We "worship" by investing our best thinking, time, efforts, finances, and emotions, committing to better our relationship with those idols. We take the God of the Bible who is all-wise and all-powerful, and we trivialize him. We make him our personal "genie in a bottle." We re-create him in our minds as our "God-On-Demand"—someone who's "there" when we need him, when life is not going as planned, and stays out of the way the rest of the time. Instead of worshiping him and knowing him and growing into servants who want to understand his mission and follow him by faith, we carefully select Bible verses out of context that confirm our conclusion that the real goal in life is for us to be happy. Instead of humbly recognizing that God is impossible to tame, we dare to demand that he get busy and keep us comfortable.

Once we've redefined God, we proceed to reduce the Christian life to a formula. "Let's see. If we read the Bible in the morning, if we pray a few prayers, if we give some money, if we go on a short missions trip to an exotic place, if we read some Christian self-help books, then life will be great." We've done our part, so God is obligated to do his part, which is:

- to give us unbelievable marriages

- to make all of our kids turn out right

- to never allow us to be depressed, or even sad

- to keep any bad things from happening to us

We've got a checklist of expectations that God must meet. But ultimately what we're saying is that we worship our own happiness. In the meantime, we've reduced God from the sovereign Lord of the universe to a servant who's supposed to fulfill our personal agenda.

So, when our cities are full of violence, our friends get cancer, our kids don't turn out right, we don't have marital bliss, and our lives are hard in this fallen world, what do we do? We have words with God. "What's the deal, Lord? I've been going to church regularly. I pray. I even put something in the offering plate! . . . Where are you, God?" We've melted him down into a modern-day golden calf. We've reduced him to a dispenser of personal peace, prosperity, and self-fulfillment.

I've got news: that's not the God of the Bible. He may give you a wonderful marriage and your kids may turn out great, but you also live in a fallen world where bad and painful things happen. The goal of worshiping Yahweh, the triune, holy God of the universe, is that he is all that there is. He's the way and the truth and the life, and we are his disciples who are to endure or enjoy whatever comes our way. He is the Creator and we are his creatures. Life is about him being at the center, not us.

We tend, by that secret law of the soul, to make a god who will eliminate all difficulty; yet the God of the Bible gives us the grace to overcome any difficulty. His promises are not easy. Jesus said, "In this world you will have trouble. But take heart! I have overcome the world" (John 16:33). I am with you, Jesus says, and I will give you peace. I will help you through the troubled marriage, the wayward child, and the chemotherapy.

I meet people all the time who are very disappointed with God because they've been taught that the Bible makes promises that it never actually makes. Actually, it promises a lot more. There's more to life than the golden calf of self-actualization and emotional fulfillment.

Salad Bar Religion

Another common effort we see in our day to reduce God is what I call "salad bar religion." Just like the Israelites, we exchange the one God worthy of everyone's worship for the many gods that mean nothing.

I remember sitting on a plane with a woman in her late-twenties. We exchanged a few pleasantries before we took off. During the flight, I opened my Bible to read a little.

"Oh, are you spiritual?" she asked.

I thought for a moment before I answered. "Well, we all have a spirit that resides in us. But there's also a vacuum in our lives that can only be filled by a relationship with the God who made us."

"Oh, wow," she gushed, "we have a lot in common."

"Well, tell me a little bit about you," I said. "What do you believe?"

"Everything," she declared.

I asked her what she meant by that.

She started counting on her fingers her beliefs. She had gathered assorted experiences from Buddhism, Bahaism, Christianity, Judaism, Hinduism, and numerous other sources to compile her own "everything" religion.

When I asked her to talk about the God she worshiped she said, "Well, God's got all this love. The heaven part I like—the hell part I don't. Stuff about judgment—I don't think God could be like that. I think he's always loving." She had created this amazing god out of the salad bar of all religions—picked what she wanted, rejected anything that did not suit her liking, and declared, "I'm spiritual."

Who is she worshiping? She's worshiping herself. She has essentially assumed, "I must be all-knowing, I must be all-wise, I must be all-powerful, and I must know all that there is to see the truth in all the different forms of people reaching for God. And I am the one who will determine what that is for me. I am the center of my universe, and I will make up all my rules so that I can be happy. Therefore, I am God." She has committed the ultimate act of reductionism by making God just like herself—and making herself her own god. And, lest any of us get too smug or critical of such arbitrary reductionism, my observation is that we all tend to do the same thing in varying degrees.

Third Focal Lens: God can only be known as he reveals himself to us!

If we're going to see God accurately, as he longs for us to see him, we've got to see him as he's revealed himself. He is not like us and he will not submit to our reductions. In fact, it's only when we recognize and encounter God—as he is—that we will then make progress toward becoming all that he has created us to be. This third lens allows us to see three primary ways God has revealed himself.

THROUGH NATURE

God reveals himself universally through nature. He has clearly written evidence of himself into the created order. Psalm 19 says, "The heavens declare the glory of God; the skies proclaim the work of his hands. Day after day they pour forth speech, night after night they display knowledge. There is no speech or language where their voice is not heard" (vv. 1–3). Everyone on earth who sees the sky, the stars, and the sunset has seen the creativity of God. Whether it's in a hut or a high-tech hospital, all of us see the miracle of birth, the order and balance in the universe. God displays speech, reality, and truth about himself throughout nature.

Paul picked up this theme in Romans 1:20 when he wrote, "For since the creation of the world God's invisible qualities—his eternal power and divine nature—have been clearly seen, being understood from what has been made, so that men are without excuse." People who insist that the world looks like an accident are simply ignoring the facts. Honest scientists are finding more evidence every day of a powerful designer behind the universe.

If you want to begin to see God with 20/20 vision, you would do well to park at a scenic spot like a beach, a canyon, or a forest, get out of your car where people aren't around, and sit down.

Set your watch for thirty minutes and observe nature. Don't try to solve anything—just look. Then go to a little park and watch young children play and laugh. See the unadulterated joy in their life, and God will speak to you. He will whisper to you what he's like. Whether it's on a slow walk in the forest, on a trip to the mountains, or while simply staring at the stars from your back porch, God displays himself throughout nature.

THROUGH HIS WORD

Observing nature will give you a true but only partial picture of who God is. Creation will stir you to know more and see better. God says if you want a clearer picture, the second place he reveals himself is through his written Word. Throughout this book you will have the opportunity to explore some of the many specific ways God reveals himself in the Scriptures. God is the original communicator and he created us as receptors of his Word. God revealed himself throughout the Old Testament as he spoke to people at various times in many ways. He communicated through dreams, visions, fire, plagues, and even through a burning bush. These are just a few of his various ways, and he didn't stop there. He revealed himself to us perfectly through his son, Jesus. Hebrews 1:1–3 tells us, "In the past God spoke to our forefathers through the prophets at many times and in various ways, but in these last days he has spoken to us by his Son, whom he appointed heir of all things, and through whom he made the universe. The Son is the radiance of God's glory and the exact representation of his being, sustaining all things by his powerful word." Jesus explained God in every possible way.

THROUGH HIS SON

God's written Word is not an end in itself. Let's continue to explore the best way in which God reveals himself: through his Son. In John

1:1–4, the apostle John wrote, "In the beginning was the Word, and the Word was with God, and the Word was God. He was with God in the beginning. Through him all things were made; without him nothing was made that has been made. In him was life, and that life was the light of men." John goes on to clearly identify Jesus as the Word: "The Word became flesh and made his dwelling among us. We have seen his glory, the glory of the One and Only, who came from the Father, full of grace and truth" (John 1:14). We're going to find later that Jesus displayed every character trait of God perfectly while he walked this earth.

When Jesus was interacting with some very religious students of the Word, he said, "You diligently study the Scriptures because you think that by them you possess eternal life. These are the Scriptures that testify about me, yet you refuse to come to me to have life" (John 5:39–40). If we don't meet Jesus Christ in and through the Scriptures, we have missed the central reason God gave the Word to us. We need to come to the Bible expecting to experience the kind of event the disciples did after the resurrection—an Emmaus experience. As they walked between Jerusalem and Emmaus, Jesus opened the Scriptures to two disciples and showed them that they were all about him (Luke 24:13–35). He will still do the same for us.

We're about to explore the truth about the God who has no place on the salad bar of religions. Jesus claimed to be God, and he demonstrated his identity by raising the dead, healing people, feeding people, and rising from the dead himself. He displayed absolute perfection, love, kindness, and holiness in perfect balance. The Word was not only made flesh; the Word was God.

John continues with his description of the Word. "For the law was given through Moses; grace and truth came through Jesus Christ. No one has ever seen God, but God the One and Only, who is at the Father's side, has made him known" (John 1:17–18). The readable revelation of God came through Moses and the other writers of the Word; the relational revelation of God came through Jesus, who has "made him [God] known." If we want to see God as he longs for us to see him, we must look at Jesus very closely.

What will it take for us to see God with 20/20 vision? First, an admission that our eyes don't see very clearly on their own. That's basically the theme of this chapter. Second, we need to take a trip to the doctor for a prescription that will correct our vision and help us see with clarity and accuracy. That's what the rest of this book is about. It's a close look at the prescription that was written out by God himself—the God who wants to be seen. He longs for our vision to recognize him for who he really is.

3

GOD LONGS FOR YOU TO SEE HIM

Before we look more closely at some of God's characteristics, let's take a few moments to evaluate our current view of God. It's one thing to say we've avoided the misconceptions about God that we listed in the previous chapter. It's another thing to sense God's eagerness for us to know him. We can claim that we don't think God is like us, that we're not trying to manage him, and that we believe he has revealed himself in nature, the Bible, and Jesus. But, having made those claims, what picture of God do we actually have? Or, perhaps this question is more personally relevant: How do I know whether or not I am seeing God as he really is?

If we accept the new lenses our spiritual optometrist prescribed for us, we will look across the room at a chart before we leave the office. Our doctor wants to make sure that every aspect of our vision is functioning at top capacity. We'll need to take a vision test.

Vision Test

In his classic *Knowing God*, J. I. Packer uses a study in Daniel to identify four measurements that help determine whether we actually know God. These by-products of godly vision can be measured on four scales:

- **Amount of energy for God.** Those who really know God have great energy for him. How much energy do you have for him?

- **Greatness of thoughts about God.** Those who really know God think great thoughts about him. What are your thoughts about God like?

- **Degree of boldness for God.** Those who really know God demonstrate boldness for him. How bold are you?

- **Level of contentment in God.** Those who really know God find great contentment in him. How content does your relationship with God make you?

Before we continue, I encourage you to take the vision test now. It will measure your current vision of God, and it will help you track your progress as you immerse yourself in God's attributes.[1]

Energy

Those who know God have great energy for God. When you have an accurate view of God, you have energy to get into his Word. When you see things that are wrong in the church, you have energy to lovingly fix them. When you see people in need, you have energy to move in for God, you have energy for prayer, and he becomes the priority in your life. If you have energy for God, you have a pretty accurate view of him. Where do you fit on the continuum today? Circle the number that represents you.

Low Energy / Vague Knowledge   High Energy / Clear Knowledge

| 0 | 1 | 2 | 3 | 4 | 5 | 6 | 7 | 8 | 9 | 10 |

Thoughts

Those who know God have great thoughts of God. When you know God, there will be times in your prayer when you will hear yourself talking about his majesty, his glory, his righteousness, his holiness, and his purity. You will sit in quiet silence, overwhelmed with his greatness. You will discover that it is possible to love God with your mind.

On the scale below, where do your thoughts about God fall? What comes to your mind when you bow your head and start to pray? Do you find your mind stimulated as you anticipate thinking about God? Circle the number that represents you.

Low Thoughts / Vague Knowledge   High Thoughts / Clear Knowledge

| 0 | 1 | 2 | 3 | 4 | 5 | 6 | 7 | 8 | 9 | 10 |

Boldness

Those who know God show great boldness for God. When you have an accurate view of God in a fallen world, you have to continually choose between what the world thinks and what God says. People who really know God are bold in their choices for God.

Among the early apostles, the greatest evidence of being filled with the Holy Spirit had nothing to do with gifts, but rather with boldness. Hebrews 11 is filled with references to great women and men of faith, and the examples used to describe them almost always have something to do with their confidence in God. Knowing God, they went boldly.

If you are bold about your convictions and are not controlled by what other people think, you have an accurate view of God. Fear of exposure indicates low knowledge of God. Circle the number that represents you.

Low Boldness / Vague Knowledge   High Boldness / Clear Knowledge

| 0 | 1 | 2 | 3 | 4 | 5 | 6 | 7 | 8 | 9 | 10 |

Contentment

Those who know God have great contentment in God. When you have an accurate view of God, you understand that he is all-knowing, all-seeing, all-powerful, and thoroughly good. He is *for* you. You can have difficulties, but you're not uptight and you're not anxious and you're not worrying because your life is under his care.

You say, "This tribulation is a struggle, but the King of the universe with all his resources, who gave his Son for me and dwells in me, will work this out. It may be hard and I may have some ups and downs, but I have a peace that surpasses understanding." Those who have great contentment in God reveal an accurate view of God. How does your present level of contentment measure up? Circle the number that represents you.

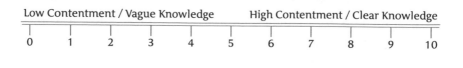

Low Contentment / Vague Knowledge   High Contentment / Clear Knowledge

| 0 | 1 | 2 | 3 | 4 | 5 | 6 | 7 | 8 | 9 | 10 |

So, how did you do? According to J. I. Packer's vision test, how well do you see God at this time in your life? Wherever you marked the line to identify your present location, add an arrow pointed in the direction you are moving. Please don't be discouraged. No matter what your "starting point" right now, I can assure you that God desires your view of him to get clearer.

The God Who Longs

God wants to see you move from knowing him dimly to knowing him vividly! He longs for distance to be transformed into intimacy. He already knows you intimately; he wants you to know him intimately too. We've already explored the *ways* God has revealed himself, but we haven't really stopped to consider the passion with which he's done so. What does it tell us about our Creator that he would go to such extraordinary lengths to make himself accessible to us?

We know God wants to know us because we have the record of Jesus's memorable expressions of longing. Scattered throughout the Gospels are numerous examples of Jesus's compassion toward others. The Bible often stretches the capacity of language to capture the depth of his feelings. John 13:1, for example, describes his emotions as he prepared for the Last Supper: "It was just before the Passover Feast. Jesus knew that the time had come for him to leave this world and go to the Father. Having loved his own who were in the world, he now showed them the full extent of his love." John tries to convey the intensity of Jesus's role as mediator between his Father and those he came to love and save. As his time on earth drew to a close, Jesus intensified his efforts to reveal his Father. Earlier that week, Jesus had expressed a broad, poignant longing of God's heart to be recognized. On the journey from Bethany to Jerusalem that became known as "the triumphal entry," a brief, almost overlooked episode captures what Jesus was thinking about all that was going on around him:

> As he approached Jerusalem and saw the city, he wept over it and said, "If you, even you, had only known on this day what would bring you peace—but now it is hidden from your eyes. The days will come upon you when your enemies will build an embankment against you and encircle you and hem you in on every side. They will dash you to the ground, you and the children within your walls. They will not leave one stone on another, because you did not recognize the time of God's coming to you." (Luke 19:41–44)

Jesus wept because they did not realize he came from God. He wept because the consequences of their blindness kept them from knowing and experiencing his peace and forgiveness. In this passage, God's longing is expressed in terms that remind us of God's faithfulness to reveal himself whether we recognize him or not. Our rejection of Jesus did not divert his desire for us. He died on the cross saying, "Father, forgive them, for they know not what they do."

Yes, the lengths God went to demonstrate his love for us can be summarized by the intimate concept of "longing." The moment the gospel helps us realize who we are and what we have done, what follows has often been called "a powerful drawing toward God" that brings us to repentance and salvation. That "drawing," seen from God's side, is his desire to be known by you and me.

What would happen in your life if you actually began to believe that the God of all time and eternity wanted you to know him? I don't mean just intellectual assent to that proposition, but an internal, emotional "awakening in your soul" that compelled you to do whatever necessary to see and know him as he is.

Two Questions

Two critical questions will emerge in your passionate pursuit of the Almighty. First, if he is indeed infinite, sovereign, eternal, and beyond all human comprehension, the question arises, "Is it really possible to know him?" And second, if he is knowable, "What must I do to know him as he is?" Let's take them one at a time.

1. Is it really possible to see God just as he is?

Can we really, in this life, pull back the curtain and the shroud of mystery and say, "I've seen all of God"? The answer is yes—and no. Yes, we can know God truly, but no, we cannot know him exhaustively. Let me explain.

The "no" part is easy to demonstrate. Notice what Exodus 33:18–20 says: "Then Moses said, 'Now show me your glory.'" Translation? Lord, I want to see all that you are. "And the LORD said, 'I will cause all my goodness to pass in front of you, and I will proclaim my name, the LORD [or Yahweh], in your presence. I will have mercy on whom I will have mercy, and I will have compassion on whom I will have compassion. But,' he said, 'you cannot see my face, for no one may see me and live.'"

So can you see all of God exhaustively—just as he is? Not if you want to stay alive. You can, however, see him to the degree he reveals himself to you, which is as much as any of us can handle.

You can receive genuine, compelling, and accurate knowledge of God. But demanding to see more of God than he chooses to reveal would simply lead to your demise. Remember, we're not like him.

And yet, God deeply longs for you to see him. John 4:23 tells us the Father is actually seeking and pursuing people to be his worshipers.

Much of the dialogue from the Last Supper in John 14 has to do with the way God has revealed himself in Jesus. When Philip finally asked Jesus point-blank, "Lord, show us the Father and that will be enough for us" (John 14:8), the Lord's answer was very revealing. You can even sense Jesus's frustration as he answered: "Don't you know me, Philip, even after I have been among you such a long time? Anyone who has seen me has seen the Father. How can you say, 'Show us the Father'?" (John 14:9). His answer is clear. You *can* know God. Jesus is the fullness of deity in bodily form. What you know of him can be 100 percent accurate. Because of who he is you can never know all of him—but all you need to know of him is in the person of Christ.

That doesn't mean God is a passive object of study for us to put under our limited microscopes. He is intimately involved in self-revelation. In fact, his *revelation* to you will depend largely on his *relationship* to you. First Corinthians 2:12 describes this basic process: "We have not received the spirit of the world but the Spirit who is from God, that we may understand what God has freely given us." It is only when you are born a second time as a result of having turned from your sin and receiving Christ as your Savior that the Holy Spirit comes in. The Spirit gives you the ability to understand what you already possess in Christ.

The next verse underscores the point that spiritual knowledge requires the Spirit's presence and assistance. Verse 14 explains why some people just don't get it: "The man [or woman] without the Spirit does not accept the things that come from the Spirit of God, for they are foolishness to him, and he cannot understand them, because they are spiritually discerned."

Some people don't get it because the Spirit doesn't live in them. They have not yet received the Spirit because they haven't yet received Christ as Savior. When he enters our life, we have new spiritual eyes. That's why Paul prayed for his Christian friends, "I pray also that the eyes of your heart may be enlightened in order that you may know the hope to which he has called you, the riches of his glorious inheritance in the saints, and his incomparably great power for us who believe" (Eph. 1:18–19). God's Spirit reveals him truly to those who believe.

Can you sense the dynamic aspects of relationship in this process? You can read the remaining chapters of this book as if they are a collection of facts about a stranger. You could get to the end of these pages and say, "Well, I think I'll be better able to recognize God if I ever meet him." Or you can anticipate each of these chapters as an opportunity to have the God of the universe draw you into a deeper and more intimate understanding of who he is. If that's your longing—to know him—then your heart is beating in rhythm with his. Read on! This, of course, leads us to a crucial follow-up question.

2. What must I do to see God as he really Is?

We have already partly answered this question in addressing the first one. How does someone "see" God? There has to be the kind of spiritual change and preparation that occurs in salvation that we just discussed. But we're not passive in that transformation. The best answer to the "what must I do" question is two words: *seek him.* "You will seek me and find me [and be able to see me]," says God, "when you seek me with all your heart" (Jer. 29:13).

Both the Old and New Testaments include promises about this process. God tells us through Jeremiah,

> "For I know the plans I have for you," declares the LORD, "plans to prosper you and not to harm you, plans to give you hope and a future [knowing that God is good, knowing he has a good plan]. Then you will call upon me and come and pray to me, and I will listen to you. You will *seek me* and *find me* when you [search for me or] *seek me* with all your heart." (Jer. 29:11–13, emphasis added)

Seeing God is not a laid-back spectator sport. It will require everything in your being, your heart, and your emotions. Your life must say to God, "I want to see you. I long to know you."

Jesus also described the process:

> Ask and it will be given to you; *seek* and you will *find*; knock and the door will be opened to you. For everyone who asks receives; he who seeks finds; and to him who knocks, the door will be opened.
>
> Which of you fathers, if your son asks for a fish, will give him a snake instead? Or if he asks for an egg, will give him a scorpion? If you then, though you are evil, know how to give good gifts to your children, how much more will your Father in heaven give the Holy Spirit to those who ask him! (Luke 11:9–13, emphasis added)

God promises you will find him if you seek him. He also promises to give you the Spirit you need in order to know him if you ask. Are you seeking? Are you asking? Are you knocking? Are you praying, "God, I want to know you"?

One of the reasons we don't know God better is our unwillingness to follow what we already know. He wants us to see him and be transformed. He wants us to experience his love, his grace, and his holiness far more than we do. But the ball is in our court. We must seek him.

"Seeking" may seem like a vague spiritual concept, but God's Word doesn't leave us in the dark. The following verses are worth highlighting in your Bible.

> [1]My son, if you accept my words
>   and store up my commands within you,
> [2]turning your ear to wisdom
>   and applying your heart to understanding,
> [3]and if you call out for insight
>   and cry aloud for understanding,
> [4]and if you look for it as for silver
>   and search for it as for hidden treasure,
> [5]then you will understand the fear of the LORD
>   and find the knowledge of God. (Prov. 2:1–5)

Each verse of that passage includes a specific action you can take in seeking God:

Verse 1. The first step of seeking God is to accept, learn, treasure, and store up his Word.

Verse 2. Step two involves submission and teachability, a desire to be taught by God.

Verse 3. Then develop a passionate prayer life. When was the last time you earnestly pleaded with God for understanding? Spent extended time alone with him? Fasted as you sought his face?

Verse 4. Make your quest for God a priority each day. Determine to meet and experience him before breakfast, work, and your daily duties. Seek after him with the same zeal with which you would search your backyard if you knew a million dollars in gold was buried there.

Verse 5. Step five provides us with motivation for a lifetime. If we seek him with all our heart, we will experience the knowledge of the Holy One.

Seeing God as he longs for you to see him means discovering the true knowledge of God. Did you notice what Proverbs 2 says? *You* will take these steps. A teacher, a pastor, or a preacher can't do it for you. You will discover because *you* dug and *you* cried out. True knowledge of God only comes firsthand. I'm sure that Tozer, Packer, and the greatest verbal painters of the character of God throughout church history would all agree that even the best description of God will never compare to knowing him personally in all his grace and glory. And the amazing fact is that God longs for you to see him exactly that way!

There's nothing more important than getting an accurate view of God, seeing him as he desires to be seen. In the rest of this book, we will hold seven attributes of God up to the light of his Word, examining them as we would examine a diamond. We'll ask God to focus our view of him with crystal clarity. These attributes are God's character traits or divine characteristics. Like seven facets of a diamond, we will think about God's goodness, sovereignty, holiness, wisdom, justice, love, and faithfulness. Each of these attributes will allow us to see God in a new light. We will glean new insight into ways God's attributes combine to affect our lives. Growing in the way we see God will also deeply affect the way we see ourselves. Like driving in my VW Beetle with Denise, you will have "aha" moments when God's Spirit helps you see yourself in ways that will forever change your life. This is a journey definitely worth taking.

Before you turn the page, I'd like to ask you to stop for three minutes. I invite you to shut your eyes and think about who God is and what he's like. If you need to, review what you read in this chapter. Reflect on the character of God and your desire to know him. Give your heart, soul, and mind an opportunity to consider who made you, who loves you, and who longs to be seen clearly by you. At the end of the time, talk to him. Ask him to reveal himself to you like never before.

Once you have done that, you will be ready to know God in an even deeper, clearer way than you ever have—exactly as he longs for you to know him.

If you have never entered into a personal relationship with God and you have questions about how to do that, I've included a guide for you in the appendix, "How to Have a Personal Relationship with God."

4

THE GOODNESS OF GOD

For the LORD God is a sun and shield;
The LORD gives grace and glory;
No good thing does He withhold from those who walk
uprightly.

Psalm 84:11 NASB

I was involved in an intense battle that no one else saw. Outwardly, I was a nice enough guy. I had cleaned up my language, I was reading my Bible, I was praying more, and I was attending church regularly. But I knew that wasn't enough. I realized that Jesus wanted to be Master of every area of my life—finances, school, sports, my future, and, as I was painfully aware at the time, my relationships with the opposite sex. He didn't just want the visible and superficial parts of me. He wanted all of me.

It was the classic battle that every believer faces. Some seem to win it quickly, and others spend a lifetime wrestling with God's authority. For me, this silent struggle raged for the better part of a year. There were several battlefronts, but the main one was my dating life. I wasn't sure I wanted to trust God to select my future mate. I considered Bible verses, listened to messages, and spent time alone in prayer, all the while hearing in the background a strong urging by God's Spirit to allow Jesus full control in my life. I knew the right answer, but deep inside I resisted it. My response was consistent: "Lord, I'd really like to hand it all over. I really would. But I just can't do it."

If someone had asked me at the time, I'm not sure I could have even put into words the struggle I was having. All I knew was that the thought of giving complete control of my life and my future over to God sent chills up my spine. Trusting God that way, that completely, filled me with dread. I imagined it would result in being single for the rest of my life. Or maybe even worse, I would be married to someone dull and unattractive, serving God in some godforsaken place infested with bugs, alligators, and snakes. I hate snakes. I couldn't see any fun in a future with God in control.

Intellectually, I knew God was in charge. He is God, after all. But I dreaded what he would do once I turned the steering wheel over to him. Would he tell me I couldn't play basketball anymore because it wasn't spiritual enough? Would he send me thousands of miles from everyone I knew and loved? Would he make chaos out of my life? Would he ask me to die a martyr's death at a young age? I knew that discipleship would cost me, and I was afraid that the cost would be too high and too painful.

God broke the stalemate in a way I didn't expect. He used a tactic for which I had no defense. Since I couldn't see him clearly where I was, he took me to a place where he could improve my vision.

One evening I had a dinner invitation from a young farmer and his wife. I was a student at a small college in a small town, where I attended a small church. I was warmly welcomed as one of the temporary residents, particularly by that young farm family. They invited me over for a home-cooked meal. College students, of course, never turn down home-cooked meals. So how could I refuse?

When I reached this family's farm out in the hills, I felt like I was driving into a Norman Rockwell painting. A huge old barn dwarfed the farmhouse. In the twilight, the glow from the windows offered a warm welcome. Inside, threadbare rugs partly covered the worn spots on the linoleum floors. The furniture had certainly seen better days. Sheets hung where doors were meant to hang. But none of that seemed to matter. Their personal friendliness and the love of their kids made this college kid immediately feel at home. One whiff of the kitchen had my mind and stomach captivated! And the food definitely lived up to its advertising. Yet even more satisfying than the meal was the circle of goodness into which I was welcomed that night.

Like me, this young family was also brand new in Christ, and they had a vibrant love for God. I saw the genuine warmth in their home, reflected in the faces of their two small children, and something happened in my heart. I found myself rethinking my life's wish list that evening: outward success seemed paltry compared to the wealth I saw in this man, his wife, and their kids.

When the meal was over, we cleared the table and shared a classic dessert: homemade apple pie and a little scoop of ice cream. As the children were nodding with sleepiness, the parents asked, "Would you mind? This is something new to us." They excused themselves and went into the next room. I watched them through the sheet hanging partly over the doorway. Mom, Dad, and the kids kneeled by the bed and prayed together. The voices of those children were filled with love for their mom and dad as they were talking to Jesus. I felt the bond of love in that family, and I sensed the goodness that filled that home. All evening I had watched electricity between this man and his wife, deeply in love with each other and clearly in love together with Someone else. Their prayers to him were humble and pure. That simple scene still moves me today.

Later, I got in my little green Volkswagen and drove down the winding roads back to our campus. I remember thinking about that wish list. "If I could choose my future, I would want that kind of family to be a part of it. But, would God allow me to have it?" My warped view of God made me think he only wanted hardship and sacrifice from me, and that he would never let me experience the things I saw that evening.

As I was praying that wish list to him on my drive home, I could almost hear his response: "Well, Chip, you know it's on my terms and not your own. I made everything, and I demand the same position in your heart that I hold in the universe. That's not too unreasonable to ask, is it? You remember I sent my Son for you as proof of my love. I've changed your life."

I responded from my misperceptions. "Well, God, I really don't want to sign the bottom of the title and be yours lock, stock, and barrel, because if I do. . . ." My mind began to run those images of what God might do if I gave him control—Africa, a dull and unappealing wife, hard sacrifice, early death . . . and even snakes. So I asked him about it. "Lord, how can I trust you with my life when I'm not sure you will do what's good for me?"

I had been memorizing Romans 8:32, and all of a sudden it dawned on me. I had been questioning God's goodness at the same time I was memorizing a verse that promises it: "He that spared not his own Son, but delivered him up for us all, how shall he not with him also freely give us all things?" (KJV). The implications of that verse sunk in so powerfully, it was almost like being born again all over again! I realized that if God had already given me his most precious gift—his Son—why would he start being stingy with me now? I remember thinking, *God, you mean I need to sign the title of my life over to you because if you love me and if you're good, then I can trust you?* He let me answer my own rhetorical question. I decided that night to make Jesus the Lord of my life because I saw God's goodness clearly. I had so focused on the cost and sacrifice of his lordship that I had totally missed the reward. Surrender is the channel through which God's biggest and best blessings flow.

For the first time, I began to realize how my wrong idea of God had undermined my relationship with him. How could I have thought that God was good and at the same time thought he would do bad things to me? God used a West Virginia family and his powerful Word to correct my vision of him. In place of my misperceptions, he put a brand-new, wonderful thought: He had good plans for me. I could trust him. He was *on my side*! His purpose was not to ignore or crush my desires but to fulfill them far beyond what I could imagine! It was one of the deepest, most radical revelations of God that I've ever been blessed with.

Years and many lessons later I realize that the root of my problem was my distorted view of God. I had not believed he was good. I falsely assumed that he did not have my best interests at heart and that a deeper commitment to him would likely result in my missing the things I wanted most. But when it came to God's goodness and his other attributes, I was wrong to rely on my vague impressions; I needed to see God clearly, as he has actually revealed himself. Coming to understand God's goodness transformed me because it transformed my view of God. I had the greatest struggle of my life dissolve in a matter of minutes because for the first time I got a glimpse of God's goodness. How about you? How do you see God? What do you think it really means when Scripture says God is good?

Defining God's Goodness

Whenever we wonder about the goodness of God, a clear definition can help us focus on what we can expect from him. English dictionaries define *goodness* with synonyms like *moral excellence, worth, kindness, disposed to the well-being of others*. God's goodness points to the high quality of his work or the beneficial effects of his character. In the English Bible, the word *goodness* often translates the Hebrew words *tov* and *tuv*, terms referring to that quality in God that causes him to bless people, deliver them, and store up future gifts for them. It implies a sense of delight in the one giving and the gift given. God's goodness is pleasant, desirable, fair, and generous. Psalm 84:11 says it well. The actions God takes and the gifts he gives us are all "good things."

These dictionary references and word studies provide a helpful start, but my favorite definition of God's goodness comes from A. W. Tozer:

> **Quick Definition**
>
> The goodness of God is that which disposes Him to be kind, cordial, benevolent, and full of good will toward men. He is tenderhearted and of quick sympathy, and His unfailing attitude toward all moral beings is open, frank, and friendly. By His nature He is inclined to bestow blessedness and He takes total pleasure in the happiness of His people.[1]

God's Goodness Revealed to Moses

God goes beyond dictionary definitions. He reveals his goodness in person. How? One of the first times he explicitly reveals his goodness is toward the end of the book of Exodus, where we catch up with Moses on a mountaintop receiving the Ten Commandments.

Moses wanted to know God. He had heard the voice in the burning bush and seen the miracles in Egypt and the parting of the Red Sea, which freed his people from slavery. God had provided water and manna in the wilderness. Moses had witnessed abundant evidence of God's power, but he wanted more—a personal, intimate knowledge of this powerful voice and miracle-working provider. So in Exodus 33:18 he said to God, "Now show me your glory." In other words, he boldly told God, "I really want to know you. I want to see you as you are."

God responded:

> "I will cause *all my goodness* to pass in front of you, and I will proclaim my name, the LORD, in your presence. I will have mercy on whom I will have mercy, and I will have compassion on whom I will have compassion. But," he said, "you cannot see my face, for no one may see me and live." (Exod. 33:19–20, emphasis added)

Moses wanted to see God's glory; but God showed him something much more accessible and less dangerous—his goodness.

The next verses describe what God did. He put Moses in the cleft of the rock, placed his hand over him, and answered Moses's request without killing him. God said, "There is a place near me where you may stand on a rock. When my glory passes by, I will put you in a cleft in the rock and cover you with my hand until I have passed by. Then I will remove my hand and you will see my back; but my face must not be seen" (Exod. 33:21–23).

But this wasn't a silent revelation. Moses recounts in awe-filled language the amazing, comforting words God spoke as he passed by:

> Now the LORD descended in the cloud and stood with him there, and proclaimed the name of the LORD. And the LORD passed before him

and proclaimed, "The LORD, the LORD God, merciful and gracious, longsuffering, and *abounding in goodness and truth*, keeping mercy for thousands, forgiving iniquity and transgression and sin, by no means clearing the guilty, visiting the iniquity of the fathers upon the children and the children's children to the third and the fourth generation." (Exod. 34:5–7 NKJV, emphasis added)

I love J. I. Packer's insights on this passage. "Within the cluster of God's moral perfections there is one in particular to which the term *goodness* points—the quality which God especially singled out from the whole when, proclaiming 'all his goodness' to Moses, he spoke of himself as 'abundant in *goodness* and truth.' . . . This is the quality of *generosity*."[2]

Have you ever thought of God looking at you and your life with all your baggage, your junk, and your ups and downs, and then saying, "I want to be generous to you. I long to give to you just what would make you happy—not because you deserve it, but because there's something about who I am that would bring me infinite joy to express that kind of generosity to you."

Packer continues: "Generosity means a disposition to give to others in a way which has no mercenary motive and is not limited by what the recipients deserve but constantly goes beyond it."[3] In other words, God never gives in order to get. His giving isn't manipulative. He sends "rain on the just and on the unjust" (Matt. 5:45 NKJV), showers of blessings that none of us deserve. God gives lavishly. Packer says that "generosity expresses the simple wish that others should have what they need to make them happy."[4]

Imagine God thinking about you that way! He does, you know. Those are God's actual thoughts about you. He feels that way toward you not just sometimes, but all the time. He thinks that way because *that's who he is*. God is infinite in his goodness, eternal in his goodness, holy in his goodness. You are the object of his affection, and because of his unique and divine nature, all that he expresses comes in an expansive, overwhelming, God-sized generosity toward you. Once you start to think of God like that, you won't want to stop!

Try to imagine how that would affect your spiritual life. If you pictured God leaning toward you with a smile of anticipation over all he longs to do in you and through you, it would be a lot easier to pray, wouldn't it? And after you've really messed up, it would be a lot easier to have a talk with someone whose intention is to bless and to encourage you because, at his very core, he's good.

> **"Generosity expresses the simple wish that others should have what they need to make them happy."**
>
> **—J. I. Packer**

Did you get that? Meditate on it as often as you need to. God is soft of heart and swift with sympathy toward you. He doesn't hold grudges. His arms aren't crossed. He is not, as I once thought, the cosmic policeman waiting to point out all your felonies and even your misdemeanors. He's cordial, open, friendly, understanding, agreeable, and sensitive to your struggle. Not only that, he longs to express his love, goodness, kindness, and compassion to regular, ordinary people like you and me. God does this not because we have been good or because we deserve it, but because he is good and he wants to. It is part of his very nature and character.

God is divinely and positively disposed toward you. He takes holy pleasure in your happiness. He is not down on you because you live in a fallen world; he is for you in the midst of it. That's how we are to define God's goodness. That's how we should think about him. Those pictures, words, and ideas are what God wants to flood our hearts and minds with as we sing about his goodness. It is better than life!

That's part of true worship. Worship is seeing who God really is and responding to that truth from your heart, your life, your time, and all that you are, because you just can't help it. You get overwhelmed with his generosity and are embraced by his goodness.

Maybe you're like I was and find it hard to believe that God feels that way about you—that he's really good, generous, waiting, smiling, and that he wants to do something good for you. That is a very foreign concept for many of us who for whatever reasons—family, background, religious baggage—have come to intuitively believe that God is always down on us, asking us to do something very hard without having our best interests in mind. Our distorted perception produces a god who looks like a menacing policeman with radar vision and no sense of humor, tapping his nightstick while he waits for us to make a mistake. Or he's like the angry parent who is always critical, no matter how well we do on our report card, always insisting that we could have done better. Those images that have infiltrated our minds keep us from trusting him. Aren't we ready for a better picture—particularly if it's true?

We can see the true picture. This God whose goodness I have been describing has actually demonstrated this part of his nature to us. He has given us proofs to demolish the wrong ideas that you and I have built up in our minds.

How Does God Reveal His Goodness to Us?

How does God reveal his goodness to regular people like you and me? Let me give you three specific channels God uses to broadcast his goodness to us.

Through Natural Blessings

First, God pours out goodness through natural blessings. I list this first because we are so prone to overlook some of the things that God does for us all the time. We fall into the subtle trap of taking for granted the order and beauty of the world we live in. We ignore the daily blessings of weather, seasons, and life that are evidence of his goodness. Storms, tsunamis, earthquakes, and natural disasters—the "acts of God" we complain about—should actually remind us of God's amazing constancy in spite of a fallen and dysfunctional world.

David was moved by God to write a hymn of praise that celebrates God's goodness and love through the created order—Psalm 145. Notice as you read it how God lavishes his goodness not just on believers, but also unbelievers and all his creatures. "They will celebrate your abundant goodness and joyfully sing of your righteousness. The LORD is gracious and compassionate, slow to anger and rich in love. The LORD is good to all; he has compassion on all he has made" (Ps. 145:7–9).

Read that last line again. Who is included in "all"? You are. Twice. That means there's nowhere in the universe you can go to get away from God's goodness. The Scriptures declare that he is good to *all*. He has compassion—deep feelings of concern—that translate into action to keep and comfort us in our darkest moments.

A little later in the same psalm, we read, "The eyes of all look to you, and you give them their food at the proper time. You open your hand and satisfy the desires of every living thing. The LORD is righteous in all his ways and loving toward all he has made" (Ps. 145:15–17).

What a great picture of God as the faithful provider! And there, waiting on the last line again, is a reminder that his goodness applies to you. It is all-inclusive. You are part of "all he has made."

Verse 21 ends the hymn with David's personal expression of worship: "My mouth will speak in praise of the LORD. Let every creature praise his holy name for ever and ever."

Did you notice that this verse ends with a command? One of the most powerful ways you can begin to believe and experience God's goodness is to continually celebrate that God is good to all. Every good and perfect gift comes from him, even the little ones. God has given us more than we need simply for survival in this world. He has given us pleasure, beauty, and meaning. Every relationship, every job, every tree, every flower, every moment is a sign of his compassion. Every corner of your world and every part of your day can remind you of his goodness if you will only begin to look for it.

Through Specific Deliverance

Another way God expresses his goodness is through specific deliverances. The Scriptures are filled with numerous examples of God delivering his people. A classic passage is Psalm 107. "Oh give thanks to the LORD," it begins, "for *He is good*, for His lovingkindness is everlasting" (NASB, emphasis added). This verse presents a theme of celebration repeated throughout the Psalms. Even a casual reader will note that this thought recurs strategically to focus not only on giving thanks but also on grasping the variety of ways in which God reveals his goodness. In fact, take a moment to open your Bible and slowly read all of Psalm 107. You may want to underline each occurrence of the phrase, "Let them give thanks to the LORD for His lovingkindness." As you read, note the four different scenarios that the psalmist uses to demonstrate how God reveals his goodness. The common thread between these events is that all of them are specific deliverances. God intervenes in crises. He meets people like you and me in acute times of need. He shows up with help for one reason—because he is good.

I've summarized the four deliverances of Psalm 107 as follows:

- God redeems the helpless from their enemies because he is good.

- God rescues us from the shadow of death because he is good.

- God heals our diseases because he is good.

- God protects us from the storms that threaten to sink our lives because he is good.

These deliverances refer to countless times in the history of God's people when he stepped in with power to save the day. Although it's true that God's plans do not always work out in ways that we would prefer, it is amazing how often we focus on the relatively few difficult circumstances of our lives and tend to forget his repeated, loving acts of deliverance that occur so regularly. As you read each section of this psalm, pause and think of a parallel in your own life. Ask God to help you remember how he intervened for good and brought about deliverance for you and the ones you love. In what ways has God specifically demonstrated his sheer goodness in your life?

One of my most vivid memories of God's deliverance was his rescue of a lifelong friend of mine. Glen was serving as a missionary in Sri Lanka. During a vacation, he took his family to an ocean resort for some rest and relaxation. When Glen was on the beach with his wife and two kids, a young man out in the water suddenly began to wave and shout that he was getting pulled under. No lifeguards were there, and it was obvious that if no one intervened, the boy would drown.

A strong Minnesota farm boy and an excellent swimmer, Glen ripped off his shirt and dove in. He cut through the pounding breakers and reached the struggling victim just in time. He dove below the boy, grabbed him from behind, and heaved him out of the undertow to the surface. His timing was perfect. A wave caught the boy and carried him toward waiting hands near shore.

But Glen's tactic put him in the clutches of the same undertow from which he had just rescued the boy. He was slammed to the bottom, pinned by an invisible hand. "I couldn't move at all, and I was completely out of air. I cried out, 'Oh, Jesus, help me.' Pictures flashed through my mind. All I could think was that my wife and two kids were going to watch me drown in front of them.

"I didn't know how I would die, but I never thought it would be like this," he continued. "I gave up. I stopped fighting. There was nothing I could do. I knew death was close. The next breath I took would be all water, and I was ready to pass out. What I expected to be my last conscious thought turned into a prayer: 'Oh, Jesus, save me!'

"Literally, as though something grabbed and threw me, I popped to the surface and a wave swept me in toward eager hands. They got me to the beach and helped me cough the water out of my lungs. When they turned me over, another missionary, Robin Cook, was there, bending over me. The dregs of adrenalin helped me sit up, but I was shaking badly. Someone threw some towels around me. After it was all over, I turned to Robin and said, 'God is good, isn't he?'"

I'm not sure how God gives people the right words for the right time, but Robin had a memorable answer. He put his hand on Glen's shoulder and said, "Glen, God sure is good, but he'd be good even if you died out there."

That's true. Ultimately, God isn't good because he does good things for us. And God isn't good because of something in us. God is good because of something in him. He can be nothing else. Both God and his choices remain good, even when they may not feel or look particularly good to you. His intrinsic eternal nature, in all of his attributes, is good. God is, in Tozer's language, "Cordial, benevolent, . . . open, frank, and friendly. . . . He takes holy pleasure in the happiness of His people."⁵ In his wisdom and sovereignty, he decides the perfect times to respond to your cries of distress, to deliver you, and to display his greatness. God doesn't have to respond at all, nor every time, nor even in the same way every time. He acts because he is merciful and because he is good. He longs for you to get to know him and trust him in a way that causes you to turn to him when you crash. Why? Because God is *for* you. He wants to bless you—generously. Once you start keeping track of God's goodness, you will find you can't keep up. His blessings through nature are countless (Ps. 145); his rescues are continuous (Ps. 107). There is no safer person to go to in the universe. There is no surer source of deliverance or blessing than God's goodness. And yet, beyond all this evidence, the apex of God's revelation of his goodness is in his Son.

Through God's Son, Jesus

As a little boy, in a heart-to-heart talk with my mother, I shared with her my thoughts about God. "Jesus is OK," I said, "but God scares me. I get the feeling that he's standing with his arms crossed, just waiting for me to mess up." I hadn't been raised in a Christian home, so I didn't know anything about the Trinity. All I knew was that Jesus came across as compassionate, and God did not.

Years later, I learned the truth. God's primary evidence, the way God reveals his own goodness most clearly, is through his Son. In fact, that's

God's pattern of revelation: Jesus is the finest example available to illustrate *any* aspect of God's character. Colossians 1 reminds us that Jesus "is the image of the invisible God" (v. 15), and that "God was pleased to have all his fullness dwell in him" (v. 19). Jesus is God's goodness in the flesh.

Mark 10 records the encounter between the rich young ruler and Jesus. The young man had it made in the shade, but he was still troubled about his eternal destiny. He realized that Jesus was a good man: raising people from the dead, teaching with great power, and living a pure life. So he came to Jesus and said, "Good teacher, . . . what must I do to inherit eternal life?" (v. 17).

He got an unexpected response: "'Why do you call me good,' Jesus answered. 'No one is good—except God alone'" (v. 18). Don't misunderstand—Jesus was not making the point in any way that he and the Father are not One. He was making the point that calling someone "good" goes further than politeness. Goodness is an absolute quality possessed only by God. The young man may have been trying to compliment Jesus's goodness as an ability, but Jesus wanted him to think again. Was the rich man ready to seriously consider to whom he was speaking? Jesus's life and death revealed, like no other person or event in all the universe, the goodness of God.

The young man's response demonstrated he wasn't serious about goodness. He was juggling "goods" in his life, and he wanted "eternal life" as another good thing to have. As the story unfolds, we learn that he rejected the absolute goodness that confronted him in order to hang on to his earthly goods.

Jesus reveals God's goodness in at least three ways. The first comes in the form of *the undeserved goodness that he gives to us*. According to

Romans 5:8, "God demonstrates his own love for us in this: While we were still sinners, Christ died for us."

God's extravagance flowed out of Jesus's heart even while you and I were his enemies. He sent Christ to die upon the cross as our sin substitute. It's unmerited goodness. You don't deserve it. I don't deserve it. He didn't do it because you said, "I'll clean up my act; I'll try really hard; I'll be a better person; I'll be more faithful to my wife; I'll be kinder at home; I'll clean up my language; or I'll be a good little boy or girl." None of those empty promises stirs God's goodness, because they are too late. The damage of sin has already been done.

God demonstrated his love toward you while you were still a sinner, a hostile rebel, an enemy of God. How? By allowing Christ to die in your place. What Jesus did on the cross shows how the Father feels about you. Have you ever considered how valuable you must be to God, given the price that he's paid for you? Have you ever just let your mind try to grasp how precious, important, desirable, and deeply loved you must be for God the Father to let Jesus die to rescue you for himself? If you can ever get a handle on that, if it ever really sinks in, it will change you deep inside.

The second evidence of God's goodness in Christ has to do with *the promise of future benefits*. Romans 8:32 says, "He who did not spare his own Son, but gave him up for us all—how will he not also, along with him, graciously give us all things?" In other words, God has already shown his goodness toward you in the biggest way possible. How can you wonder whether he'll take care of the details?

God loves you; he wants you to know he's good. But you share a basic problem with the rest of humanity: we all have a warped view of God. When it comes to God's goodness, as with all of his attributes, the wrong view always produces a strong, negative emotional response. We will not recognize God's goodness as long as we're convinced he has other intentions than our welfare.

God, fortunately, isn't waylaid by our misperceptions. He sent his Son, Jesus, to die in your place and mine, thereby offering the ultimate proof of his goodness and love. He now persists in catching our attention through a thousand little details that he takes care of in order to give us continual glimpses of his goodness.

My evening at the farmhouse was one such glimpse. God used Romans 8:32 to utterly transform my view of him. The cross, God's radical sacrifice in Christ, is the clearest and most compelling evidence that God has my best interest in mind. The logic is airtight. If God has already loved us enough to give us his very best, don't you think he has the best in mind for our future? Put in simple terms, if someone paid a million-dollar ransom to free you from a kidnapper, do you really believe you'd have to worry about who's going to buy lunch the next day? My point is that God's generosity in the cross reminds us that not only has he been good to us, but also that he is committed to being good to us in the future. That is why we can trust him when those big lordship decisions come up. We can surrender ourselves to him because he is very, very good.

How Are We to Respond to God's Goodness?

God's goodness requires a response. But if we have lived with an inadequate view of God for a long time, we may not even know how to start. There are specific steps we absolutely must take to change our lives and begin to fully experience the effects of God's generosity.

Repent of your unbelief and ingratitude.

Romans 2:4 says, "Or do you despise the riches of His goodness, forbearance, and longsuffering, not knowing that the goodness of God leads you to repentance?" (NKJV). Paul was asking, "Do you think that all the good that came in your life was because you're an incredibly nice person who made God's special list? Has he been doing this for you because you deserve it?" The answer to that would be—no!

God wants you to know that he has been good, kind, cordial, loving, and generous with you to lead you to repentance. He has been drawing you with goodness, not threats. The word *repentance* means "to have a change of mind," or "to turn around." It means that you're going down the road and you realize, "I'm going the wrong direction. I'm doing my things my way for me. I need a change of mind, a new direction. I need to go God's way." So you take the off-ramp, you go over the overpass, and then you take the on-ramp going in the opposite direction. That's repentance—a turned-around life. We are to see God's goodness and have a change of mind that leads to a change of direction that leads to a changed life.

The Bible talks about repentance and faith together. They go hand in hand. If you're not a believer in Christ right now, God's goodness can lead you to the point where you say, "God, I'm sorry I have not recognized that all the good, all the kindness that's come into my life is from you. Please forgive me of all my sin. I want you to know that I'm turning back your way. I'm going to embrace your Son. I ask you, Jesus, right now, to come into my heart, forgive me of my sin, and save me forever." The goodness of God drew you to him, and he will accept your prayer.

But even for a believer, repentance and faith are crucial. Perhaps like me, you entered the Christian life with some twisted, distorted view of God. You believe, but you don't really *trust* him yet. Even now, my life sometimes gets infected with discontentment and thanklessness. When God gives me nine, I want ten. When he gives me ninety-nine, I want a hundred. No matter what the blessing, we manage to be ungrateful. No matter what God does for us, we always say, "I want a little bit more."

When God's goodness shows us this condition in us, it should lead us to repentance and faith. We need to say, "Lord, I've been thinking wrongly about life. I've gotten all into the gifts instead of the Giver of the good gifts. I want to become, little by little, in my heart, one of the most thankful people on the face of the planet. I want to give thanks to you in the morning, I want to give thanks to you at noon, I want to give thanks to you under my breath. I want to revel in the flowers, the trees, my relationships, and all that I have, not obsess about what I don't have. I want to thank you for my salvation. I want to thank you for your Word, for your Spirit, for your good plan for my life. God, I want to be the kind of believer that would make it easy for you to smile down upon with holy pleasure because you see that I recognize that all I have comes from you."

Rest in his goodness when you encounter adversity.

We know that life is hard. You didn't need this book to tell you that we live in a fallen world. Bad things happen to good people, and good things happen to bad people.

Psalm 31:19–20 says:

> How great is Your goodness,
> Which You have stored up for those who fear You,
> Which You have wrought for those who take refuge in You,

Before the sons of men!
You hide them in the secret place of Your presence from the con-
   spiracies of man;
You keep them secretly in a shelter from the strife of tongues.
(NASB)

Sooner or later, most of us face situations that are out of our hands. We walk through the valley of the shadow of death. A loved one lies suffering or dying. All we can do is wait and pray. How does God's goodness help us then? We can't deny that it's a fallen world. We *know* death may come. Though we know God has the power to reach in and revive our loved one, that may not be his good plan. But we are called to rest in his goodness anyway. And we can. We've been given promise upon promise that his goodness underlies everything he brings us through.

One of the goals of my life is that I will habitually give thanks as an unconscious response to all circumstances and all relationships in light of the goodness and sovereignty of God. I've got a long way to go, but that's my goal. I want one day for my unconscious response to be gratitude, no matter what the news is and no matter how difficult circumstances seem. I want to know instinctively that whatever he has allowed to come into my life has come through hands that are kind, cordial, and benevolent.

I don't know all the specifics of God's will, but I do know how great is his goodness that he has stored up for me and my house, for all those who take refuge in him. In your adversity, rest there. He's an eternal God with an eternal plan. He doesn't always work things out this side of heaven the way you want him to, but you can count on this reality: he is good.

Risk stepping out in faith like never before.

When we discover that God is good, we will find ourselves taking ever-increasing steps of faith. For me, recognizing Christ as the Lord of my life represented a significant risk. But as soon as I made that choice, I began to discover God's goodness in ways I couldn't see before. God's goodness reinforced my small steps of trust. He didn't ship me off to some far-off place I did not want to go to or condemn me to a boring life. On the contrary, because I grew increasingly confident that God had a good future in store for me, I found myself excited about new days and fresh opportunities to experience him. That monumental decision about Christ's lordship led me to entrust my entire future to him.

Trusting in God's goodness transformed my definition of risk. It allowed me to take the "risky" step of turning down a great job in order to move and start a ministry on a college campus in West Virginia. At that campus I met a wonderful woman named Theresa, who became my wife and with whom I now share four children and eleven grandchildren who are in turn experiencing God's goodness. Over thirty years of ministry has broadened and deepened my awareness of God's goodness. I now realize that even those things I feared God might ask me to do actually could have been positive because he has consistently shown me he will not ask me to do things that are not ultimately good for me. When you and I believe that God is good, we will be able, like never before, to take the risks of actually living by faith.

I don't know what specific steps of faith God is prompting you to take right now, but there is one Bible passage in particular that has served as an expression of God's goodness when I'm faced with decisions involving risk. That passage is Psalm 84:11, and it's one of my favorites. In fact, I carry it on a card to remind me of this priceless truth: "For the LORD God is a sun and shield; the LORD gives grace and glory; no good thing does He withhold from those who walk uprightly" (NASB).

Meditate on those words for a moment. The Lord God is a sun. What's the sun? It's a resource, power, sheer energy. The Lord is a shield. What's a shield? A protector. How would you like to have an infinite, all-wise, good, loving, kind, unlimited resource and protector? "The LORD God"—his covenant name and title, the name he uses to sign his promises—"The LORD gives grace and glory." That's comprehensive. He lavishes us with unmerited favor, kindness, goodness, and blessing.

And then, the clincher. What a promise! *No good thing* will he withhold from those who walk uprightly. You'll never miss out if you do life God's way. Walk uprightly in your sexual life, in your relational life, in your financial life, and in your spiritual life. In other words, if you do life his way, the God who is on your side with unlimited power, unlimited wisdom, and unlimited compassion gives you a guarantee: he'll make sure you don't miss out.

When you clearly see God's goodness, you start taking steps of faith. You do crazy things like giving up your vacation to go to Romania to help orphans. You start giving money to people who need it a lot more than you do. You attempt things that used to scare you to death, like talking to others about God's goodness. And then what will God do? He will pour goodness into your life and love and relationship and finances. When you exercise faith you begin to experience God's goodness at a whole new level.

My Experience with the Goodness of God

I was a young pastor with only a few years of experience under my belt. When people came to me for counseling, I was often at a loss to know what to tell them. On one occasion, I found myself talking to a young woman who had just been through a messy divorce. Her husband had left her for another woman. His actions during the divorce had damaged both his wife and their children. I hoped our church would be able to help her in some way, but I wasn't at all sure that I could offer her much comfort.

As we talked about her future, she displayed a sense of calm that caught me by surprise. She hadn't been a Christian very long, and she didn't have an impressive amount of Bible knowledge. Her life, in fact, had been marked by repeated experiences of extreme pain and disappointment. But when I asked her about her outlook and her concerns for her children, she answered in an unexpected way.

"I know life may be hard," she said, "but things will be great for my children and for me. I don't understand it all, but I know what God is like. I know he would never do anything to hurt me, and I know he has a great plan for us."

It wasn't so much the words she said—although they were profound—but the sense of confidence that flowed with her statement. She wasn't someone who had learned "Christian clichés" or felt compelled to tell me how she ought to think. It was almost as if she had just walked out of an adjoining room where she had enjoyed a personal conversation with God, who had assured her that all was well. Her posture and tone of voice carried genuine calmness. Based on her understanding of God's character, she was convinced that her future looked bright even though her present was filled with pain and questions. She knew something more real than her immediate suffering.

I remember that conversation vividly, though it happened over three decades ago. Her response became one of many that have underscored for me again and again that our view of God is the most important thing about any one of us. This young woman's biblical knowledge may have been limited, but what she knew was pure gold. She understood with all her heart that God is good. I think of her and others like her as beautiful trees standing in the middle of a harsh, desert landscape. Everything around them looks ruined, yet they thrive. They are so alive that they look out of place. It's only when I glance closer that I realize they are filled with life because their roots tap into an underground river—the goodness of God.

Live It Out—B.I.O.

"Bio" is a word that is synonymous with "life." Found in those three simple letters, B.I.O. is the key to helping you become the person God wants you to be.

B *Come BEFORE God daily.* Meet with him personally through his Word and prayer to enjoy his presence, receive his direction, and follow his will.

I *Do Life IN COMMUNITY weekly.* Structure your week to personally connect in safe relationships that provide love, support, transparency, challenge, and accountability.

O *ON MISSION 24/7.* Cultivate a mindset to "live out" Jesus's love for others through acts of sacrifice and service at home, work, play, and church.

Come BEFORE God

• Write the following definition on a notecard, smartphone, or tablet and read it when you get up in the morning and when you go to bed. Don't try to memorize it. Simply read it in a spirit of prayer and let the reality of God's goodness gently pour over your soul.

The goodness of God is that which disposes Him to be kind, cordial, benevolent, and full of good will toward men. He is tender-hearted and of quick sympathy, and His unfailing attitude toward all moral beings is open, frank, and friendly. By His nature He is inclined to bestow blessedness and he takes holy pleasure in the happiness of His people. . . .

The whole outlook of mankind might be changed if we could all believe that we dwell under a friendly sky and that the God of heaven, though exalted in power and majesty, is eager to be friends with us.[6]

A. W. Tozer

- Near the definition, write Psalm 84:11 and meditate on that promise. Each time you read it, begin by asking, "What good thing has God released into my life today?"

  For the LORD God is a sun and shield;
  The LORD gives grace and glory;
  No good thing does He withhold from those who walk uprightly.
  Psalm 84:11 NASB

- Join me in making the following prayer your own for the next seven days:

  O Lord God, full of goodness and mercy, as I look into the face of Jesus and ponder the goodness of the cross, help me to

  - *repent of my unbelief and ingratitude,*

  - *rest in your goodness even in the midst of trials, and*

  - *risk trusting you in every area of my life like never before.*

I praise you that I live under a friendly sky, that you are for me, and that I need never be afraid of the future because you are good.

In Jesus's name, Amen.

- What lie about God's goodness have you believed?

Do Life IN Community

- Create a gratitude list. Take a few minutes each day this week to write down specific ways God has been good to you. Thank God for being good and for all the ways on your list.

- Share a few of the ways God has been good with a friend or family member.

Be ON Mission

- When you clearly see God's goodness, you start taking steps of faith. What risky step of faith has God prompted you to take?

- God used a family in rural West Virginia to help me see his goodness. Who has God used to help you see his goodness? In what tangible way can you show the goodness of God to someone this week?

5

THE SOVEREIGNTY OF GOD

This is what the LORD says—
    Israel's King and Redeemer, the LORD Almighty:
I am the first and I am the last;
    apart from me there is no God.
Who then is like me? Let him proclaim it.
    Let him declare and lay out before me
what has happened since I established my ancient people,
    and what is yet to come—
    yes, let him foretell what will come.
Do not tremble, do not be afraid.
    Did I not proclaim this and foretell it long ago?
You are my witnesses. Is there any God besides me?
    No, there is no other Rock; I know not one.

Isaiah 44:6–8

Why do you think your God is better than all the other gods?"

It was an honest, fair question, not argumentative in the least. I was on a plane from Hong Kong to Beijing, surrounded by people whose language I couldn't speak. My wife and daughter were seated about twenty rows back. I had been surprised by the articulate British voice coming from a thoroughly Chinese-looking person in the seat next to me, and I had begun to talk to her about my relationship with Christ. And this cultured, well-manicured, highly intelligent woman honestly wanted to know: "Why is your God better than the rest?"

As we talked, I found that she had grown up under atheistic communism, spending the first twenty years of her life being taught that there was no god at all. She was one of the elites, among that 1 or 2 percent— out of a billion or so Chinese—who scored high enough on academic tests to get the finest education her country offered. After graduate school in London, she began working in England for a multinational corporation and was now back in China on business. Out from under communism, she had been reading for the last ten years about various religions and beliefs. When it came to various religions' views of God, she was virtually a clean slate.

What do you tell someone who knows hardly anything about your God? She had a legitimate question, and I gave it my best shot. For the next two hours, I shared passages of Scripture and research from archaeology, philosophy, and comparative religions to help her understand the absolute uniqueness and character of the God of the Bible. I told her everything I could think of to explain why the God of Christianity is in fact Lord of lords, King of kings, and Creator of the universe.

As this woman had already discovered, we live in a pluralistic culture that tells us to be tolerant of all concepts of truth. I believe that tolerance is a very good thing, but it has been misapplied. As it is defined in the dictionary, tolerance has to do with accepting other people's race, background, culture, and other externals, making sure that these things will not be a deterrent as we relate to them. That's a very important thing to emphasize in our society. But tolerance has taken on a philosophical meaning in recent years; it has evolved to mean that no idea or view is any more true or valid than another.

Although this concept carries a certain air of intellectual sophistication and openness, think of how it might apply to other areas of life. What if, for example, you had a life-threatening infection and you went to a doctor for help. Suppose the doctor prescribed penicillin, but one of the nurses suggested several alternatives. How would you feel if the nurse advised the doctor to be open to all the options? After all, Coumadin, Cytoxan, and morphine are all very effective drugs. Isn't it intolerant of the doctor to prescribe one drug over the other? Maybe so, but you wouldn't want him to be indiscriminate when one drug will save your life and the others will not, would you?

"I'd like a drink of water with two parts hydrogen and two parts oxygen, please."

"Sorry, that's hydrogen peroxide—not exactly a thirst quencher."

"Okay, how about one with just two parts hydrogen."

"Well, don't sit near someone smoking."

"Why?"

"You'd be inhaling some highly flammable gas. Ever heard of the Hindenburg?"

"How about three parts hydrogen and one part nitrogen, would that soothe my parched throat?"

"No problem."

"Really?

"Yeah, if you like ammonia."

Water is defined as two parts hydrogen and one part oxygen.

Regardless of personal preferences, scientific credentials, alternative constructs, distaste, or even disdain, you can't change the building blocks of water. Once altered, you have a very different substance.

In our culture's laboratory of tolerance, people want to mix and match their ideas about God and hope it turns out to be God. For many, the idea of a sovereign or all-powerful God cannot be fused with a God who seems to allow free rein for evil. Unfortunately, regardless of personal preferences, scientific credentials, alternative constructs, distaste, or even disdain, you can't change the building blocks of God. Once altered, he ceases to be God.

Isn't that narrow and bigoted? We know, of course, that such a view would be disastrous. When it comes to objective reality, being tolerant doesn't cut it. Some things simply aren't relative.

But, like many in our own country, that's the kind of culture my Chinese acquaintance was living in. She had been told that all truths are equal and valid. And I found myself telling her a story about a God who had saved my life and about a God-man named Jesus who made some really outrageous claims. She had every right to ask me: "How do you know?"

I think a lot of people are asking the same question she asked me. At the time, I hoped and prayed that I gave her some pretty solid answers. But if I had it to do over again, I might present a more thought-out case for the God who is sovereign.

Why Worship This God?

If I had another opportunity to answer this woman, who was so open and sensitive, I would say this: The reason I believe in the God of the Bible and worship him is because he is *before* all things, he *created* all things, he *upholds* all things, he is *above* all things, he *knows* all things, he *accomplishes* all things, he *rules over* all things, and he is *in control* of all things. That's the reason I believe him and have given my entire life to him in faith and in trust that he is superior to all the other truth-claims in the world. He is not just another "-ism" out there to be considered. He is infinite and eternal, over all and worthy above all. I worship him because he is *sovereign*.

On the salad bar of the world's religions, we haven't simply come up with a nice little system that takes a little bit from here and a little from there. Our God is not just one option among many. We worship a God who has made outrageous, ridiculous, exclusive, "narrow" claims about himself. He insists that he, and he alone, is to be worshiped.

Think about what God says of himself. (Scripture references have been added for further study, and I'd recommend sitting down with a cup of coffee sometime and going through these one by one.)

- He is **before** all things; all things hold together in him. He was there before the mountains were born, he brought forth the earth, he is the Alpha and Omega, and he alone is immortal (Ps. 90:2; Col. 1:17; 1 Tim. 6:16; Rev. 1:8).

- He **created** all things, both in heaven and on earth, both visible and invisible (Gen. 1:1; John 1:3; Col. 1:16).

- He **upholds** all things, sustaining everything, holding it together by his Word (Col. 1:17; Heb. 1:3).

- He is **above** all things, specifically so that people in China, the US, South America, and everywhere, may know him (Isa. 45:5–12; Eph. 4:6).

- He **knows** all things. He isn't a limited God. God knows everything completely before it happens (Ps. 139:4, 6; Isa. 46:10).

- He **can do** all things. Nothing is too difficult for him! Nothing—not anything—is impossible with him (Jer. 32:27; Luke 1:37).

- He **accomplishes** all things. He orchestrates and determines what he is going to do in your life, in my life, in the president's life, in war-torn countries with rebellious rulers—everywhere! Whatever he plans in this world and for this universe, he does (Isa. 14:24; 46:10; Eph. 1:11).

- He **rules over** all things. This is what sovereignty is. All strength and power are in his hands (1 Chron. 29:11–12; Dan. 4:34–35).

- He is **in control** of all things. Whenever the economy goes sour, or whenever earthly kings rage out of control, God is in control. When Satan wants to mess with your life, he has to ask God's permission (Job 2:3–6; Rom. 8:28).

If you want specific examples of what exactly is under God's control, take a look at the following verses:

- earthly kings (Prov. 21:1; Rev. 19:16)

- human events (Ps. 33:9–11; Dan. 2)

- good angels (Col. 1:15–16; Rev. 4:8)

- Satan and fallen angels (Job 1:6; Eph. 1:21; Phil. 2:10)

- human decisions (Acts 2:23; 13:48; Rom. 8:29–30; Eph. 1:11)

God makes numerous claims about himself in the Bible that many other religious systems don't even attempt to rival. When he claims his sovereignty, he is pointing to himself as the ultimate source of all power, authority, and everything that exists.

What Does That Mean?

I don't know about you, but the first time I heard the word *sovereign*, it didn't register with me. I was a new Christian in a Bible study in college, and some tragic news had come to us about a member in our group. One girl in the Bible study said, "I know it's a terrible situation, but I know God is sovereign." And being the smart, intelligent, spiritual guy that I was, I thought to myself, *What in the world does that mean?* I had never heard the phrase "God is sovereign" in my life. So later I went to a close friend and asked him to explain it to me.

This may surprise you, but one of the greatest tools for Bible study is the dictionary. Webster's defines sovereignty like this:

> **sovereign—adj.** 1: above or superior to all others; chief; greatest; supreme 2: supreme in power, rank, or authority 3: of or holding the position of ruler; royal; reigning 4: independent of all others 5: excellent; outstanding—**n.** 1: a person who possesses sovereign authority or power; specifically, a monarch or ruler.

If someone is sovereign, he's the boss. He calls the shots and has the authority. What he says goes. He's "the king." God claims to be the King, not just of this planet, but of the entire universe. He is outside of time. He is infinite. He had no beginning, he has no end. He is the ruler of everything.

When I think of sovereignty, the phrase I like best is that "God is in control." That's such a comfort. When a loved one lies in a hospital bed, God is in control. When we think of our most difficult times with a child, God is in control. When a close friend is in ICU, God is in control. When the economy—national or personal—is on a slide, God is in control. Nothing will enter your life that God does not either decree or allow. And nothing will ever enter your life that, if you are willing to trust in him, he cannot work out for your good. That's what it means to be sovereign.

Because God is sovereign, he is without equal: the King of kings, the Lord of lords, without limitation in any way. He is the only *absolutely free* being in the universe. I love A. W. Tozer's explanation of sovereignty in his book *The Knowledge of the Holy*:

Quick Definition

God's sovereignty is the attribute by which He rules His entire creation, and *to be sovereign God must be all-knowing, all-powerful, and absolutely free.* The reasons are these:

Were there even one datum of knowledge, however small, unknown to God, His rule would break down at that point. To be Lord over all creation, He must possess all knowledge. And were God lacking one infinitesimal modicum of power, that lack would end His reign and undo His kingdom; that one stray atom of power would belong to someone else and God would be a limited ruler and hence not sovereign.

> Furthermore, His sovereignty requires that He be absolutely free, which means simply that He must be free to do whatever He wills to do anywhere at any time to carry out His eternal purpose in every single detail without interference. Were He less than free, He must be less than sovereign.[1]

When you bow your head to pray—when you're in a jam and you need to ask God for something—are you aware of whom you're talking to? The one to whom you pray has power over the entire universe, over every single atom, and yet he is infinitely loving and he cares about you. *That's* who you're talking to. That's why we worship him.

Can you imagine what my Chinese friend might think of this idea? It was an utterly foreign concept to her. And behind her polite dialogue and earnest questions, I could hear her heart saying, "I know *you* believe what you just told me, but I'm going to need more evidence than you've given me if *I'm* going to believe." As our conversation progressed at 33,000 feet, I could hear in her voice both the longing to know and the fear of making a mistake and believing the wrong thing. She wanted to let go of her childhood world without God, but she wasn't sure which of the gods being offered to her was the best or true alternative. She understood the implications of belief—it would have to lead to obedience and worship. As I looked into her eyes, I could almost hear her say, "If what you're saying to me is true, that there is someone who loves me and has the answer to all my problems, I want to get to know him. But I need more evidence. How has the God of the Bible, if he exists, revealed his sovereignty?"

How Has God Revealed His Sovereignty?

Intellectually, my friend didn't have a problem with the sovereignty of God. I mean, who wants to believe in a helpless, impotent god who may care but can't do anything to help us because he isn't in charge? But emotionally and spiritually, she wanted to know God's sovereign credentials. Both of us had been required to show our ID in the airport before boarding the plane. She was asking me if the God of the Bible had any ID she could look at.

The Bible is God's traveling papers, his documents that demonstrate his sovereignty. There is a lifetime of information in those pages that will deepen your understanding of who God is, but let me point out five key areas in which God has revealed his sovereignty.

Through His Titles

First, God has revealed his sovereignty through his titles. The world is full of rival religious systems and ideas, but step back for a moment and think about the way other religions present their gods. On one extreme, impersonal mechanisms and forces are in charge, using methods like reincarnation to recycle us until we no longer exist. On the other extreme, there are the personal gods of "the religious salad bar" that end up as a slightly larger version of the believer, easily altered by that believer if the god in question doesn't satisfy.

Contrast this with the bold, personal, complex claims of the God of the Bible. These claims are so outlandish that they are either complete lies or essential truths for everyone to grasp. God says about himself:

- I am sovereign.

- I am the Most High.

- I am the Alpha and the Omega.

- I am the King of kings and the Lord of lords.

- I am who I am, the eternal, self-existent one.

- I will be addressed in reverence because of my own greatness.

These are unequivocal claims. They set him apart and do not allow us to see him as just one of many gods.

Through His Promises

The second way God reveals his sovereignty is through his promises. Anyone can make promises; not everyone can keep them. God's promises, as comprehensive and ultimate as they are, can only be kept if he is, in fact, sovereign. Consider the following two promises, for example.

The first is the promise we count on in my family whenever there's a crisis. We have quoted it often. "We know that in all things God works for the good of those who love him, who have been called according to his purpose" (Rom. 8:28). That's quite a promise! Amazingly, God can somehow take all the events, all the situations, all the people, the doctors, the medicines, the prayers, the relationships—everything involved in whatever difficult situation we're in—and work it together for the good of those who trust him. He could never stand behind that promise unless he knew *everything*. Unless he had unlimited power, was all-wise, had created everyone, and could dictate what happens down to every atom and molecule. You simply cannot work all things for good unless you are the sovereign King of the universe. But God makes that promise, and millions throughout history have testified to its truth. It's a testable claim, and God has proven his ability to back it up time and time again.

99

The second promise is found in Philippians 2:9–11. There will come a day when every knee of those who are seen (us) and those who are unseen (angels) will, at the name of Jesus, bow before him, and every tongue will confess that he is Lord. He makes that promise. How in the world can he make a ridiculous promise that every tongue will confess and every knee bow, unless he holds all power over history, both its visible and invisible aspects? The very promise is a claim to be sovereignly guarding and directing history toward his own ends.

Through History

Third, God makes his sovereignty known through "his story"—history. As you open the pages of Scripture, you see the story of a nation called Israel. Early in the pages of Genesis, God reveals that history—not just of Israel or the world, but yours personally—is under his sovereign control. For an amazing glimpse of how God works, find a quiet corner and read Genesis 37–50. More than 25 percent of the first book of the Bible is dedicated to the story of one man who gets raw deal after raw deal, but finds that the Lord was sovereignly orchestrating even the most painful and unfair circumstances in his life for his good and to fulfill God's purposes.

God lets Joseph suffer difficulty after difficulty, including being sold into slavery, put into prison, betrayed, and forgotten. But God moved Joseph into a unique position through those difficulties—into Egypt by the treachery of his brothers and into prison by the treachery of Potiphar's wife—so that Joseph could interpret Pharaoh's dreams and be elevated to the second highest position in the land. Why? Because years and years earlier, God had made a promise to Abraham. He said he would make Abraham's descendants as numerous as the sand of the sea and the stars of the sky. He would multiply the descendants of a one-hundred-year-old nomad who had a ninety-year-old wife. (You'd better be sovereign if you make a promise like that.) Abraham had a son, as promised, and Genesis 37 picks up with Joseph when we're much further down the road of this family's history.

When his family was about to die in Canaan because of a famine, God provided. God had already used all the evil and repeated injustices of others to place Joseph in a strategic position in Egypt so that the seventy family members would come down and find food and life. Through God's sovereign plan in Joseph's life, Egypt became this family's incubator until they had multiplied to two or three million people in fulfillment of God's promise.

> "You intended to harm me, but God intended it for good to accomplish what is now being done, the saving of many lives."

After Joseph's father died, the brothers were very concerned—with good reason, considering their treachery—that Joseph was now going to kill them. But in Genesis 50:20 he turned to his brothers and gave us the classic biblical testimony to God's sovereignty over a personal and national history: "You intended to harm me, but God intended it for good to accomplish what is now being done, the saving of many lives." What did Joseph believe?

That God was sovereign. Even when he was sold, put into prison, betrayed and forgotten, God was in control.

God wants you to know that he is sovereign in your history. When your ex-spouse says something that bothers you, when your kids do something that troubles you, when there's a problem at work, or when the market goes down, there is a God who is in total control. He is all-knowing, all-wise, generously good, infinite in his love. He's the King, and you're his child.

God not only reveals his sovereignty in personal history, he also reveals it macroscopically—over all of history. Great examples of that are found in chapters 2 and 7 of Daniel and also in the book of Revelation. There you will see God revealing his sovereignty in history by telling his prophets the kingdoms that will come. He tells Daniel specifically, "I want you to know that Babylon is going to fall, and after that the Medo-Persians are going to come in, and after that the Greeks will take over, and after that Rome will take over, and by the way, I want to give you a few details. Alexander the Great will take over, and when he dies there will be four kingdoms." God lays out the next four dynasties and kingdoms before they happen. He's in charge of history. God has never sat around biting his nails, wondering what Attila the Hun, Pol Pot, Hitler, or Osama Bin Laden was going to do. He does not sit on the edge of his seat unsure of what Kim Jong-un, ISIS, or home-grown terrorists are going to do. And you don't have to wonder either. Sovereignty doesn't mean that we should choose to be ignorant or passive about cruel injustices in the world, but it does mean that we can have a sense of peace and trust because the world is not spinning out of God's control.

Through Fulfilled Prophecy

One of the most amazing testimonies to God's sovereignty is his ability to tell the future 100 percent of the time with 100 percent accuracy. Look at Isaiah 44:6–8:

> This is what the LORD says—
>   Israel's King and Redeemer, the LORD Almighty:

> I am the first and I am the last;
>> apart from me there is no God.
> Who then is like me? Let him proclaim it.
>> Let him declare and lay out before me
> what has happened since I established my ancient people,
>> and what is yet to come—
>> yes, let him foretell what will come.
> Do not tremble, do not be afraid.
>> Did I not proclaim this and foretell it long ago?
> You are my witnesses. Is there any God besides me?
>> No, there is no other Rock; I know not one.

Did you notice the top of God's business card? "King and Redeemer, the LORD Almighty." And then he proves it by telling the future. He is not an alternative religion that you might subjectively want to choose over Hinduism, Buddhism, Islam, Jehovah's Witnesses, or Mormonism. He lays down a challenge that no one can rival: "Let him foretell what will come. . . . Did I not proclaim this and foretell it?"

A third of the Bible is prophetic. Several hundred prophecies were fulfilled in Christ. God wants you to know that you don't have to put your brains on the shelf to believe the reliability of Scripture; you can know objectively that whatever he has said he has also fulfilled. Jesus fulfilled hundreds of specific prophecies regarding the day he was born, the place he was born, who his mother was and what kind of woman she would be, and more—all to demonstrate and prove that he is the sovereign King. And there's another set of promises you need to remember about his return. He will bring history to a close. Instead of being the suffering servant who died in your place on a cross, he will then be the ruling warrior on a white horse, and he will bring about justice. He wants his people living in anticipation of the day of his return.

There are plenty of areas in which to study the power of biblical prophecy, but consider this one: can you name any people group in all of history, that, after being pushed out of its land, has kept its identity? Think that through. We talk about European Jews, American Jews, and Arab Jews. How have they kept this identity? It was foretold, and God has fulfilled his promises. God said that after his people had been spread abroad for almost two thousand years, he would bring them back into their land again; and in 1948, Israel became a nation. Thousands of years after God's prophets spoke about the return of Israel to its Promised Land, where are the eyes of the world? They are on that tiny strip of land. The prophetic evidence is amazing.

Through Jesus Christ, the Messiah

As you might expect, God's clearest demonstration of his sovereignty comes wrapped up in his Son, Jesus. Consider the phrase in Galatians 4:4, for example—that Jesus came "in the fullness of time." When Jesus was born, there was a unique set of conditions that the sovereign God of history had brought about. Greek had become a "universal" language. Travel and communications were at an all-time high. The *Pax Romana*, the Roman-enforced peace, allowed for rapid evangelism. Synagogues had been dispersed all over the Roman Empire so that when the church was birthed it would have strategic centers of operation.

Jesus clearly identified himself as the sovereign King (Matt. 28:18; Rev. 19:16). Even in his death, no one killed him against his will. We can't get mad at the Romans or the Jews; according to Jesus, no one took his life from him. He laid it down on his own initiative (John 10:18). He hung on that cross not by nails but by his choice because you matter and he loves you.

Then there's the resurrection. That's what cuts through everything else in the world of religious claims. He died and then he rose from the grave. He remained on earth for forty days after his resurrection. Jesus didn't just tell one eyewitness who then claimed a vision and asked everyone to buy into his beliefs. There were five hundred eyewitnesses who saw him, touched him, and heard him speak. At least a hundred and twenty watched him ascend into the clouds. The resurrection is not a nice story that is optional for Christians; it is a historical fact that demonstrates the authority of Jesus. Christ is the crowning glory of God's revelation of his sovereignty.[2]

If I could have that conversation again with my Chinese friend, I would have explained some things differently. If she could read the last several pages written here, I think she would eagerly do some personal research and actually look up the passages that give evidence for God's sovereignty. My experience is that, unlike people who have grown up with Christianity and often accept the evidence at face value, those who come with an open mind and actually search the Scripture for themselves discover that God speaks to them personally and powerfully. Conviction comes when you have a hunger in your heart and a desire to dig into God's Word. The Spirit of God takes the Word of God and does something in you that births faith.

If you will take the time to examine God's evidence, he will birth that faith in you. God will reveal that he is far bigger, more powerful, more loving, and more in control than you ever imagined. As you begin to see God as he longs for you to see him, your prayers will change and your faith will be transformed. You will experience peace like never before.

God's Sovereignty Raises Two Questions

Anyone who thinks about God's sovereignty long enough will face two pretty big questions. The first is this: If God is really in control and above all things, sovereign over all of history's circumstances, why does he allow evil, pain, and suffering? If he can see all the unspeakable things people are doing to each other, and if he can do something about it, why doesn't he? Why didn't he stop the world's suffering before it began?

This is a huge question that enormous amounts of literature have addressed throughout the centuries. There's simply no way to discuss such a deep issue in such a short space in a way that is fully satisfying. Those who want to explore the issue further may want to check out a good book on the issue of evil, such as C. S. Lewis's *The Problem of Pain*, for one example. But at the risk of oversimplifying, let me give what I think in a nutshell is the gist of what the Bible says on the subject.

Why didn't God prevent suffering? Because he created us in his image. The high price tag for a loving relationship among people is freedom. Human freedom means we have the willful opportunity to say yes and to love God, but we also have the willful opportunity to say no and to do what is wrong. God thought it was so important to maintain our dignity that he gave us the opportunity to freely love or reject him, knowing that our freedom would result in pain. But he allowed it, knowing before the foundation of the earth that the only remedy for that pain would be Jesus—he would come and die to pay the price that restores that relationship.

The second question regarding God's sovereignty is about human responsibility. If God is sovereign over all people and events in history, doesn't that make a sham of human responsibility? Is God a cosmic puppeteer who lets us think we're making decisions on our own? Are all our decisions predetermined, such that he is pulling the strings and making our choices an illusion?

Of course not. The Bible clearly teaches that God is sovereign, but we make decisions of our own free will. We will be rewarded, held accountable, and judged for those decisions. But there's a balance. We don't understand exactly how that works, and people who try to explain it generally fall into one of two major Christian camps—Calvinism or Arminianism (named after two sixteenth-century figures of the Protestant Reformation, John Calvin of France and Jacobus Arminius of Holland). Within those camps, many people take their explanations further than Calvin or Arminius would have taken them. Without going into a lesson on these two important figures of church history, I'll simply say that there are extreme views within those two camps that are unbiblical. Some extreme forms of Calvinism, though well-intentioned, guard God's sovereignty so protectively that it virtually eliminates human responsibility. No one who holds this belief would state it that way, but that's how it plays out. It makes God a cosmic puppeteer and denies that we have any real choices. That's unbiblical. At the other end of the spectrum are extreme forms of Arminianism. Also out of good intention, these attempt to guard free will and human responsibility so protectively that it creates a God who is up in heaven biting his nails, hoping everything will work out, and waiting for our decision so he can figure out what to do. Both extremes violate Scripture.

Scripture teaches a tension between the two. God is absolutely sovereign. No plan of his can be thwarted, and he is in control of all people, events, and history. But the Scripture also teaches that we are free, moral agents who make decisions, and those decisions can impact things for eternity. How those two truths go together is a mystery. (For interested readers, *Chosen But Free* by Norman Geisler deals with this issue in a balanced and biblical way.) Either extreme will land you in a theological ditch. But what amazes me is that the apostle Paul, who wrote so much about God's sovereignty, didn't seem to have a problem with this balance. In Philippians 1, when he was thinking he might die, Paul said he was certain that his deliverance would occur because of the church's prayers (human responsibility) and because of the provision of the Spirit in Christ Jesus (sovereignty). In chapter 2, he tells them to work out their salvation with fear and trembling (human responsibility) because it is God who is working in them both to will and to desire his good pleasure (sovereignty). Like two telephone poles that hold their wires in tension, at one end you are responsible, and at the other, God is sovereign. One brings great comfort, the other great responsibility.

How Do We Respond to a Sovereign God?

Bow before the King of the universe.

Think of the implications. If there is a sovereign King over all the universe, the first response would be to bow before him. The day will come when every tongue will confess him and every knee will bow in submission and surrender. For those who trust in Christ while alive on this planet, it will be a joyful day of awesome celebration. And it will be a day of horror for those who have stiff-armed God and said, either passively or with active rebellion, "I'll be the king of my life, I'll call the shots." Why? Because he's the sovereign King who has provided a way, and a person who has willfully chosen to reject that way has rejected him. Out of respect for our dignity, the consequences for anyone who says "I want my way" will be God's consent: "You can have it."

What's the practical application? Absolute surrender of all that you are and all that you have. That has profound implications for both the unbeliever and the believer. For the unbeliever, it means acknowledging all your sin, self-will, pride, and inability to know and love God on your own terms. It means giving your life over to Christ and following him as Lord.

For the believer, absolute surrender means that what you once thought of as *your* time, *your* money, *your* talents, *your* career, *your* sexuality, and *your* interests, is all his. It means that you turn your ideas and philosophies, your plans and your future, your dreams and your abilities over to him. It means you are no longer yours. You've been bought by the One who made you.

Is there anything in your life that you have not submitted to the sovereign Lord? Does he hold the same place in your heart that he holds in heaven and in the universe—and that he'll hold forever? Is there any barrier between you and the King? Have you surrendered your time? Your future? Your relationships? Your money? Your will? What God wants from you is a living sacrifice.

Remember the old movies, when the king would come by and the serfs would bow down in honor? Why would they do that? Because they knew that the king had the power to take their life, if he chose to. They dared not offend him. But we're not talking about a human; we're talking about the sovereign Lord, the King of glory. The wisest, most intelligent move you can ever make is to surrender all that you are and all that you have to the One who loves you like no one else can ever love you and who is in control.

Believe all that comes into your life is either allowed or
decreed by a good God who will use it for your benefit.

The second appropriate response to a sovereign God is to believe. Think about what his sovereignty means for your circumstances: all that comes into your life is either allowed or decreed by a good God who will use it for your benefit. The present conflict within your marriage? God will work it for good. The present trials with your children? God will work them for good. The present situation with the stock market, your retirement, your emotional pain and hurt, your depression? Believe that everything that has entered your life—any circumstance or relationship—has been divinely allowed or decreed by him to work it out for your good. And the good that he wants more than your circumstance or your happiness is that you be conformed to the image of his Son. All those things you're looking for—love and joy and peace and patience—these are the fruit of the Spirit working in and through you in the midst of your life's circumstances. His sovereignty ensures it.

Oswald Chambers turned God's sovereignty into a foundational principle: *Absolutely refuse to worry.* Your retirement is going down the drain? Keep working, but refuse to worry. You've been working on your marriage and are not making any progress? Pray intensely, but refuse to worry. Someone is lying in ICU? Refuse to worry. I've seen devastating circumstances, some of the worst situations imaginable, cause supernatural breakthroughs in relationships and open up opportunities for people to share Christ with power and effectiveness. God is doing things that you don't understand, things that are deeper and better and more wonderful than you imagined, but you must believe! Refuse to worry. You can stop trying to manipulate situations and trying to figure out how to make them work out because you know who is in control. You can rest in his sovereign goodness.

Behold in awe the mystery and majesty of his kind, compassionate, just, and sovereign rule over all that is or will ever be.

The third application is to behold in awe the mystery and majesty of his sovereign rule. We don't do this very often. We're more likely to say, "I don't understand it; I can't figure it out." But God's sovereignty should prompt us to worship.

I'm always interested when people argue about God's sovereignty and treat each other like heretics because another Christian doesn't believe exactly the same thing about it. Paul, whom the Spirit of God inspired to pen chapters 9–11 of Romans, gets to the end of this great passage of looking at God's sovereignty, and what does he do? Does he declare his theological position and tell everyone in the church that they need to agree with him? No, he sees the mystery of God's sovereignty and says:

> Oh, the depth of the riches of the wisdom and knowledge of God!
> How unsearchable his judgments, and his paths beyond tracing out!
> "Who has known the mind of the Lord?
> Or who has been his counselor?"
> "Who has ever given to God,
> that God should repay him?"
> For from him and through him and to him are all things.
> To him be the glory forever! Amen. (Rom. 11:33–36)

He worshiped. He broke out in praise. A proper understanding of God's sovereignty doesn't bring about arguments. It brings about awe and wonder and the bowing of the heart that says, "I'm a small, finite little person. I can't put it all together, and I hurt in a fallen world. But I

111

worship the Creator, the sovereign King, who has made me the object of his affection."

I think back to my acquaintance on that airplane from Hong Kong to Beijing. I can still see her business suit, her fine jewelry, and her carefully tended appearance. I can still hear her fluent English, her intelligent comments, and the sincerity in her voice. And I can still hear her question: "Why do you think your God is better than all the other religions out there?" It's a fair question, and I wish I could go back again and answer it in a way that truly reflects the mountains of evidence that God has given us throughout history and through his Word: He is before all and above all, infinite and wise, all-knowing and all-powerful. He is sovereign.

My Experience with the Sovereignty of God

In 1990, I made one of the biggest lordship decisions of my life. I had been a pastor in rural Texas outside of Dallas for the previous eight years, and I knew God was up to something new in our future. I prayed he would send us east, closer to family and support, as one of my teenage sons was going through the beginning of a rebellious streak.

God's call came, and it was west, not east. We moved an additional two thousand miles from all our family. Theresa and all four kids were crying as we pulled out in our van for the long drive to our new life. They didn't stop crying until Amarillo. We were obeying the clear orders of the King, but emotionally it felt terrible. I was the family leader taking everyone away from friends, family, and all that was familiar. How could a good God let obedience to his will feel so terrible? The adjustments were hard, the new church presented challenges I'd never faced, and my rebellious son became more rebellious. Where was this loving, good, and sovereign God now? I felt so alone, so confused, and often deeply discouraged.

Fast-forward twenty years. The new church and its challenges developed skills, character, and a ministry beyond my wildest dreams. The adversity brought a deeper unity into our family and took our marriage to a whole new level. The rebellious son did a "one-eighty" and had opportunities in music that were nonexistent in Texas. God built a family, grew a church, launched a radio ministry, and turned a rebellious son into a Christian songwriter and worship leader for God's people. What felt like disaster, and what seemed so unfair, was the good hand of a sovereign God working out his highest and best purposes for my life and my family.

So how about you? What are you going through that feels hard, unfair, depressing, or impossible? What would it look like to stop fighting, stop resisting, stop complaining, and start trusting your sovereign heavenly Father?

Live It Out—B.I.O.

"Bio" is a word that is synonymous with "life." Found in those three simple letters, B.I.O. is the key to helping you become the person God wants you to be.

B *Come BEFORE God daily.* Meet with him personally through his Word and prayer to enjoy his presence, receive his direction, and follow his will.

I *Do Life IN COMMUNITY weekly.* Structure your week to personally connect in safe relationships that provide love, support, transparency, challenge, and accountability.

O *ON MISSION 24/7.* Cultivate a mindset to "live out" Jesus's love for others through acts of sacrifice and service at home, work, play, and church.

113

Come BEFORE God

- Write the following definition on a notecard, your smartphone, or tablet and place it where you will read it when you get up in the morning and when you go to bed. Don't try to memorize it. Simply read it in a spirit of prayer and let the reality of God's sovereignty gently pour over your soul.

> The sovereignty of God is that which separates the God of the Bible from all other religions, truth claims, or philosophies.
>
> When we say God is sovereign, we declare that by virtue of his creatorship over all life and reality, his all-knowing, all-powerful, and benevolent rule, that he is in fact the Lord of all lords, King of kings, and in absolute control of time and eternity. Nothing will come into my life today that he did not either allow or decree for my ultimate good.

- Near the definition, write Romans 8:28 and meditate on that amazing promise. Then write Genesis 50:20 in the same note as a reminder that your present circumstances and difficulties don't tell the whole story. Each time you read it, begin by asking, "What good thing has God released into my life today?"

> We know that in all things God works for the good of those who love him, who have been called according to his purpose. (Rom. 8:28)

> You meant evil against me, but God meant it for good in order to bring about this present result, to preserve many people alive. (Gen. 50:20 NASB)

- Join me in making the following prayer your own for the next seven days:

O Sovereign Lord, King of all creation, Lord of all that is visible and invisible for all time and eternity, grant that I might this day

- *allow you to hold the same place in my heart that you hold in all the universe. Teach me to submit to your wise counsel and command even as the angels of heaven do so with joy and delight.*

- *so fully believe that you are both good and sovereign that I would absolutely refuse to worry, knowing you are working all things for my good today—even those things I don't understand and that seem so unfair.*

O Sovereign Lord, thank you for Jesus, who by his willful death and supernatural resurrection has defeated death, sin, and Satan, both now and forever. I confess you, Lord Jesus, as my King, my God, and my faithful Friend and Savior! Amen.

- What present circumstance in your life is causing you anxiety and worry? Are you trying to manipulate and control the situation? In what ways?

- Give your worry to the King of the Universe and surrender to him. Ask God, who is good, to help you believe that he has allowed this circumstance and he will use it for your ultimate good.

Do Life IN Community

- Read Colossians 1:16–18. "For by him all things were created: things in heaven and on earth, visible and invisible, whether thrones or powers or rulers or authorities; all things were created by him and for him. He is before all things, and in him all things hold together. And he is the head of the body, the church; he is the beginning and the firstborn from among the dead, so that in everything he might have the supremacy."

- What do we learn about the supremacy and sovereignty of Christ in this passage?

- Surrender to Christ is one of the ways we respond to Christ's sovereignty. Who do you need to ask to help you in your journey to live a life of total surrender? Get together with a friend and ask them for help, and then spend time praying together.

Be ON Mission

- Is there anything that God is calling you to do that requires you to surrender?

- Spend some time praying and reflecting on that question. Then, obey whatever God reveals to you.

6

THE HOLINESS OF GOD

Make every effort to live in peace with all men and to be
holy; without holiness no one will see the Lord.

Hebrews 12:14

What comes to mind when you think about the word *holy*?
Perhaps you think of monks and candles? It could be uncomfortable pews and a loud voice from the pulpit. Maybe
a walk in the forest or by the ocean comes to mind. For some, it might
be the big game or a favorite show that cannot be interrupted. Big black
Bibles and long, flowing robes are the mental pictures I used to have
whenever someone spoke of holiness. I met people who said they were
holy, and I just thought they were weird. I'm not sure many people are
very clear on what the concept means. The problem with that is that if
we don't know what God's holiness means, we'll never know where to
begin when he tells us his holiness means we should be holy. I am going
to share four specific stories from my childhood that will shed some
light on this concept of holiness. Don't try to find exact parallels with

spiritual truths in these stories. What I want you to notice are some common denominators that have helped me get my arms around this high and lofty concept.

The Jersey

He led me quietly down a dark, echoing hallway beneath the gym. This skinny sophomore was being taken on a tour in the depths of Lincoln High School, and this was a hallowed hall. It led to a wire-cage door, behind which was a washer, a dryer, and a strong smell of bleach and detergent. This holy of holies was spotless and well-guarded. Not just anyone could get in here. But I was with the varsity basketball coach.

On the far wall there were two shelves, the top one covered with neat stacks of blue uniforms and the lower one with white uniforms. Every jersey was folded to show part of a blue and gold number. Coach picked up a uniform, unfolded it, and let me hold it.

The material felt light and airy. "This is SandKnit," he whispered, "the best they make." As I ran my fingers over the number on the shirt, he told me that out of fifteen hundred students, only twelve each year would get to wear that uniform and represent the Mighty Lions.

I was bug-eyed with awe. "If you work hard and dedicate yourself," coach continued, "and if you stay focused, there is a good chance that you might get to put on one of these uniforms." He paused to let that sink in, and then stated what I already knew. "That means something around here." Then, as if to add to the mystique of the moment, he gently took the uniform back and said as he replaced it, "After you wear it, you'll never take it home. The moment you go into the shower,

we wash and fold them and they go back on this shelf. These uniforms
are reserved for a select few to wear with honor. They never leave the
building."

The Uncrossable Aisle

The ends of the huge A-frame sanctuary were covered in stained glass.
Suspended on wires from the ceiling, a highly polished cross, maybe
twenty-five feet in height, hung over the altar. The pews that filled
the room were divided down the middle by a wide aisle that lined up
directly with the cross.

Every time my parents took me to church, I would observe a familiar
ritual. My mother would get to the aisle, turn toward the cross, and
stop. She would solemnly bow and then slide over into one of the pews,
kneel down, and pray.

Being an astute little boy, I watched as each person came into the aisle,
looked at the cross, and bowed. Some even made the sign of the cross.
Even on Saturday when the custodian dusted the pews, each time he got
to the aisle, he stopped, bowed, and then he went on cleaning.

I decided there was something about this aisle. You never crossed it until
you bowed toward the altar and the cross. This was serious business.
There was a mystery about it that even affected an ornery, mouthy little
boy like me. Sometimes when my parents were distracted, I played tag
with my friends in the sanctuary. Our mad dashes across the room were
strangely interrupted by a brief stop and a nod to the altar every time
we crossed the center aisle—always. We dared not, for reasons we didn't
understand, step into the aisle without the proper respect.

The Once-a-Year Glass

We arrived home from the late Christmas Eve service after midnight. The carols were still ringing in my ears and I had enjoyed the decorations and candlelight atmosphere in the church. I was amazed that I understood the songs.

Back home, my mother had prepared heaping plates of cookies and breads, trays with cheese and meat, and all kinds of special sweets. The presents were piled under the tree, waiting to be opened. Our home tingled with mystery and excitement.

Between these expected family traditions of church services, special meals, and gift exchanging, another event always stood out. Each year, Mom would bring out a tray with tiny, long-stemmed glasses filled with champagne. I was only eleven or twelve years old and amazed I got to drink real alcohol. That was cool. But I wondered, as I tipped my glass, where it went the rest of the year. Those glasses were never used for any other occasion. Once each year with my family on Christmas Eve, surrounded with tasty treats and tempting presents, I got to drink a special potion. No other time of the year was like that brief moment.

A Ring in the Mouth

I was six or seven years old, traveling with my family on a long car trip. I was lulled by the miles into a bad mood. Those were the days before child-restraint seats, so I was free to roam. I leaned over the front seat, bothering my mother and father. My dad told me for about the tenth time to sit back down, and I responded with a very rude "No." As I watched for my father's reaction, I was oblivious to a blur of movement on my right. Mom's hand came up in an instinctive response to my blatant disrespect, bouncing her class ring off my front teeth and my lips.

Stunned more by the suddenness of her action than the pain she caused, I sat down with tears in my eyes and shock on my face, instantly chastised. Now you have to understand, my mother was an awesome, caring, tender woman. I had absolutely no abuse in my family before or after that event, which made her reaction all the more memorable. There wasn't a shred of doubt in my mind that I had provoked and deserved that response. And I'm sure she felt terrible. We didn't speak for maybe an hour. But I had just learned that there was a marked-off boundary around how I spoke to my father. Disrespect would not be tolerated. I had violated that invisible limit and received instant, painful consequences. In terms of rebellion and respect, I never crossed that line again.

How We Understand Holiness

What do the stories above have in common? Which ones, if any, shed light on your understanding of holiness? Whether or not you have ever thought seriously about holiness, you probably have some concept of what it means. Is holiness about robes, candles, and strange actions? Is it about laws and strict rules? Is it about special people, places, or certain times? When we say God is holy, or when we say he wants us to be holy, what do we mean?

The dictionary offers definitions like "to divide," "to mark off," and "to set apart from all else" to describe the uses of the word *holy*. It's the opposite of profane, common, or ordinary. To be holy is to be different, distinct, or unique. The English roots refer to that which is whole, healthy, happy, sound, complete, and unspoiled. The word *holy* eventually came to mean "spiritually pure, sacred, untainted by evil, sinless."

When applied to God, holiness is that which divides him from everyone and everything else. It is the quality of "awesome mystery" in God's being, his essential nature and character that make him different, distinct, and unique from any other thing or person in the universe.

We see this illustrated in the Bible after God parted the Red Sea and Moses wrote a song to remind the people of Israel about this invisible God who delivered them. The people had already seen the cloud, the pillar of fire, and the walls of water that allowed them to pass. Then they saw those same walls collapse and cover their enemies. Moses reviewed these startling events in his song and reached a climax with rhetorical questions: "Who among the gods is like you, O LORD? Who is like you—majestic in holiness, awesome in glory, working wonders?" (Exod. 15:11).

The answer to Moses's questions is, of course, "No one!" But note some of the words he used to describe God's uniqueness. The first is *majestic*. The Hebrew word literally means "expanded" in holiness. Whatever we see or know about God is magnified when we look through the lens of holiness. Other things may reflect God's holiness, even as your reflection in a mirror says something about you. But your reflection isn't you. Anything we use to illustrate God's holiness can go no further than the way we use a mirror to illustrate ourselves. God's holiness, like his other attributes, is in a category by itself. He isn't six or ten or one hundred times more holy than the best person you know. God himself is an entirely different category in which he is the only member.

God's holiness refers both to his majesty and his moral purity. In addition to his greatness and his "otherness," holiness includes the absolute absence of evil in his character. It encompasses and defines all that is pure, whole, righteous, and healthy in the universe. God's holiness deserves our awe, reverence, and respect.

A. W. Tozer describes this attribute of God in this way:

Quick Definition

We know nothing like the divine holiness. It stands apart, unique, unapproachable, incomprehensible and unattainable. The natural man is blind to it. He may fear God's power and admire His wisdom, but His holiness he cannot even imagine.[1]

Tozer reminds us that we can't, with our finite resources, get our arms or our minds around the absolute, sinless, majestic purity of the Creator of the universe. Even with God's help, we will be overwhelmed by his holiness long before we understand much about it.

God is holy, he is other, he is different. In his difference he is purely love, purely moral, and without sin. All that we can imagine or grasp about health, life, peace, and beauty comes under the holiness of this God who is so different than anyone or anything that we know.

That's the conceptual side of it. How should God's holiness, though ultimately incomprehensible, impact your life and mine? The towering fact of his holiness leaves us with two crucial questions that we will seek to resolve in the remainder of this chapter:

- How does God reveal his holiness so that you and I can grasp it?

- How can you and I effectively reflect God's holiness in the world?

How Does God Reveal His Holiness?

Exploring God's holiness is not just a nice way to learn more about God. There are responsibilities that flow from deeper understanding. Our exposure to God's holiness must lead to a clear reflection of it in our lives. Every person who understands enough to have Christ living in him or her can hear God say, "Do not be conformed to the former lusts which were yours in your ignorance, but like the Holy One who called you, be holy yourselves also in all your behavior; because it is written, 'YOU SHALL BE HOLY, FOR I AM HOLY'" (1 Pet. 1:14–16 NASB). God reveals his holiness in at least seven ways: through people, through places, through the law, through the prophets, through his wrath and judgment, through his Son, and through his church.

Revealed through People

Three towering people in the Bible—Moses, David, and Isaiah—offer us great examples of the way God's holiness impacts a person's life.

God called Moses out of his wilderness training ground to lead Israel through that same wilderness. From within a continually burning bush, Moses heard a voice saying, "Take off your shoes because you are on holy ground." Moments before, that corner of the desert had been nothing but dirt. Now it was a holy place. What made the difference? God's presence. In that moment with Moses, God was not simply "present" as he is in all creation at all times; God was personally present in a way that required Moses to acknowledge him. There's a spine-tingling awe and reverence when we realize that God is present. That privilege ought to cause us to remove our shoes, bow our heads, and whisper praise.

David is called a man after God's own heart. He received promises not only for his own life, but forever. He was told one of his descendants would always be on the throne, up to and including the Messiah who would rule permanently. Beginning with 2 Samuel 11, there is example after example of God's holiness in the face of David's repeated sins and shortcomings. God maintained his holiness with David both in the way he holds the king accountable for sins and in the way he deals graciously and impartially with David. God does not betray himself when he deals with his people. No matter who we are, when we are unfaithful, we violate God's holiness and there are consequences. God's holiness ensures that these consequences come with justice, grace, and love.

Another classic Old Testament character is Isaiah. Life was falling apart for Judah when King Uzziah died, and prophets were critical in such times of transition. Because prophets represented God to the people and the people to God, Isaiah turned to God in prayer for guidance and a message. Instead, he got something beyond what he ever dreamed—he was brought face-to-face with the holiness of God.

The prophet describes his life-changing encounter in Isaiah 6:1–7. He doesn't try to describe what he saw of God himself; he describes God's robe and the angels who are clustered around the throne. The angels are crying, "Holy, holy, holy is the LORD Almighty!" In Hebrew, repetition represents maximum quality. God is holy, holy, holy, and no one else comes close. Suddenly, it didn't matter that Isaiah was a prophet, a counselor of kings, or a great writer—his cover was blown. He screamed, "Woe is me! I can't be here!" The crisis of a dead king was nothing like this. Meeting God is never a casual event.

When we begin to see God for who he really is instead of who we make him out to be, the experience starts upward and then moves inward. We see God and then we see ourselves. When we get a high view of God, we stop comparing ourselves to others because we understand how much we fail to measure up to him. Instead of trying to figure out how close we can get to sin without actually sinning, we begin trying to figure out how we can get as close to his purity as possible.

As exhilarating as it is to truly see God, seeing ourselves usually starts with terror. This is why we need to know God's goodness in addition to his holiness. When we realize that he sees us clearly and completely—warts, wounds, and wickedness—that truth overwhelms us, and like Isaiah we cry, "Woe is me! I can't be here!" But we are there! God, who is great in his holiness, is equally great in other attributes. He lets us know his holiness so we might realize how much we need his love and compassion.

That's exactly what Isaiah experienced. "Then one of the seraphs flew to me with a live coal in his hand, which he had taken with tongs from the altar. With it he touched my mouth and said, 'See, this has touched your lips; your guilt is taken away and your sin atoned for'" (Isa. 6:6–7). Right after the prophet's inward realization of God's holiness and his own sinfulness he received an inner transformation.

But the process wasn't quite complete. Isaiah's transformation wasn't designed to remain inward. "Then I heard the voice of the Lord saying, 'Whom shall I send? And who will go for us?' And I said, 'Here am I. Send me!'" (Isa. 6:8). This is why an accurate view of God is so critical. An upward, accurate view of God, high and holy, leads to an inward, accurate view of yourself as fallen short and desperately needing God's forgiveness, which in turn leads to an outward view of your life being about God's agenda instead of yours, and your life being about the needs of other people instead of you and your little world.

Revealed through Places

When God reveals himself in a certain place, that place becomes holy. We saw this in God's visit with Moses through the burning bush. During the Exodus, God filled the wilderness with holy places repeatedly, revealing himself through the crossing of the Red Sea, the continuously blazing pillar of fire by night and cloud by day, the extended encounter with the nation at Mount Sinai. The people camped around the holy mountain while Moses went up to meet with God. God gave Moses instructions for constructing the tabernacle—a large, moveable tent that represented and held God's presence among his people. It was a holy place, set apart for God's use. No one was permitted to enter without special permission. Presuming on God's holiness was dangerous. Only those prepared to take God's holiness seriously were allowed to enter parts of the tabernacle.

Years later, when Solomon built the Temple in Jerusalem, he had to follow a strict order of preparation that would lead up to God's descent and filling of the magnificent structure. The intricacy and beauty of the Temple faded into the background as God's holiness filled the place.

If we fast-forward to the New Testament, we read about the church gathered for the single purpose of worship (Acts 4). They were thanking God for the privilege of suffering when the place where they were meeting began to shake. The holiness of God filled the space, and they responded with boldness in speaking the Word of God to the world.

Finally in Revelation 4 we come to a description of God in the context of heaven, the ultimate holy place. The apostle John tries to describe the indescribable. Startling and strange creatures gather around the throne of their Creator crying, "Holy, holy, holy is the Lord God Almighty, who was, and is, and is to come" (Rev. 4:8). This unending round of praise echoes what Isaiah reported in his vision, but in the clear air of heaven, the song must reverberate through the soul of everyone who is listening.

Here on earth, special places are designated as holy because God has made himself known there. Heaven is more than a holy place; it's a holy environment. Experiencing God's holiness in the little places of this world serves as part of our training for the real holy land of heaven. Whenever God is present and wherever he reveals himself, be it a beautiful temple, a desert bush, or in heaven, that place automatically becomes holy.

Revealed through the Law

God has revealed his holiness through the law. The first four of the Ten Commandments deal specifically with his holiness. Since God alone is truly holy, we are to trust and worship no others. We are not to dishonor God's holiness by pretending anything or anyone else is God. His name should be used with utmost respect and care. When he declares a holy day (the Sabbath), it is holy. The summary of God's laws focuses our attention on his holiness.

This principle is demonstrated in painstaking detail in the first five books of the Bible, particularly Leviticus, in which God spells out the specifics of worship. It's easy to skip Leviticus when we're reading through the Bible. It wasn't until I began to treat God's holiness seriously that I also began to study the ceremonial washings, the sacrifices, the rules about circumcision, and the dietary instructions. I discovered these laws were not arbitrary; they were given with reason, because the Designer knew things about life that people wouldn't discover for centuries. Long before we understood about E. coli, bacteria, and the spread of disease, God gave his people rules that prevented serious epidemics. A modern study uncovered the curious fact that the blood of newborn boys reaches a particularly high capacity for coagulating on the eighth day—the day God set apart for circumcision. Who would have known? A holy God would.

All of God's laws are reflections of his holiness. Why do you think he gives believers in our day very explicit instructions about purity in sexuality? Because we matter. We're wandering in a cultural and moral wilderness as real and dangerous as the wilderness Israel walked through. As he did with them, God has given guidelines and boundaries to make sure we get the very best sex, to make sure we don't get diseases, and to maintain very clear boundaries. God says one man, one woman, and one relationship, for life together. It worked then and it works now, but we have a world (and a large part of the church) that has abandoned God's design, and with tragic consequences.

I meet Christians all the time who say, "I just don't do that one." "What do you mean you don't do that one?" I ask. "I, you know, I believe the Bible, I asked Christ to come into my life, but the sexuality one, I think it's kind of Victorian. I just don't obey that one." Do you realize what that says about our relationship with God? Have we come to the day where we pick and choose which commands we'll obey because we're so superior and we're so unique and we're so different, and we're so wise we should tell God what's best for us? Our words don't say it like that, but sometimes our actions do.

Revealed through the Prophets

Isaiah represents a special group God chose as his representatives. God not only revealed his holiness *to* prophets, he revealed his holiness *through* them. A prophet's job was simple: get the truth from God, primarily about his holiness and his benefits, and then give it to people in a loving and powerful way. The prophets' messages may have varied, but their themes remained consistent. They confronted Israel's tendency to worship idols. Prophet after prophet cried out, "Stop going after other gods!"

What were the idolatrous people violating? God's holiness. They were treating him with the salad bar mentality. But God will not settle for divided loyalties and part-time worship. He will not accept a role as one among many or even the best among many. He is in a holy category by himself. Just as husbands and wives expect full-time commitment from each other, God expects full-time commitment from his people. That is why idolatry is often described as spiritual adultery in the Bible.

That's how God views spiritual unfaithfulness. That was his repeated message through the prophets.

Revealed through His Wrath and Judgment

When people refuse to listen to the warnings of the prophets, God reveals his holiness directly through wrath and judgment. The effects are sudden and devastating. They have an eerie similarity to what I experienced with my mother when she instinctively reacted to my blatant disrespect for my father. It was a wake-up blow that achieved its intent. I had not heeded the warning signs, so the judgment was swift. Even as I sat there stunned, I knew she had done it because she loved me and simply wasn't going to stand for me dishonoring my relationship with my dad.

Likewise, God's wrath is his just anger toward anything that would destroy or damage what he has created and loves. When we see judgment in the Bible, we can be sure that it falls because God cares so much that he guards and enforces his holiness.

In the book of Joshua, God gave Israel clear directions about what to do with Jericho's possessions after the fall of the walled city. A man named Achan coveted the silver, gold, and clothing he saw collected from the city. Although he knew God's guidelines, he blatantly disobeyed and stole what he wanted. As a result, the nation suffered a defeat and Achan's entire family died. Pulled out of context, God's wrath and judgment may appear harsh or unfair. At such moments, we risk setting ourselves up to pass judgment on God. His holiness apart from his other attributes can certainly inspire fear and awe. It ought to. Unless you and I come to understand God's holiness, we will not appreciate how his grace and mercy intervene on our behalf.

We see this same pattern in the New Testament with Ananias and Sapphira in Acts 5. They chose to make a mockery of other believers, God's holiness, and the privilege of giving when they lied about their gift. They treated God as someone they could fool. God, everyone discovered, will not be mocked.

God loves us so much that when we choose to step outside of the boundaries of his holiness, certain consequences act like a vise to bring judgment into our lives to correct us until we say, "I yield." If you are hardheaded like me, the experience can be tough because the vise often gets very tight before I even start paying attention. God often uses our finances, our circumstances, and our relationships. He'll target our emotions, our job, and our family. He will do whatever it takes to get as much of our attention as he needs to say, "Be holy, for I am holy."

My basketball coach probably didn't realize he was helping me understand holiness by the way he taught us to respect the uniforms we wore. Those articles were set aside for special work and treated with honor. Coach would have been outraged if any of us borrowed a team jersey to wear in town. He would have interpreted such an act as an extreme insult that profaned the name of the school. A player who did that would have been benched or kicked off the team. Why? Because if those uniforms became casual clothing, they would lose their value as reminders of the privilege and responsibility we had as members of the team.

One of the ways the Bible describes the life of a believer in Jesus involves the phrase "putting on" our faith in Christ (see Eph. 4:20–26). As Christians, we bear his name. On the back of our jerseys it says "Follower of Jesus." As his representatives, the way we live tells other people what we really think of him and his words, and it also helps compel them toward Christ or repel them from him. When people see us live in a way that is not consistent with God's Word, that is serious business to God. His Son's reputation is at stake. Our lives honor or dishonor him. Disrespecting God's holiness leads to wrath and judgment, because God's true character will be revealed one way or another.

Revealed through His Son

As with his other attributes, the most complete revelation of God's holiness comes through his Son, Jesus. From start to finish, Jesus's life illustrated, proclaimed, and proved God's holiness. For a key example, read about the transfiguration in Mark 9:2–13 during which Christ unveiled his glory and holy light shone from him. The disciples saw the glory of God and they realized Christ was fully man and fully God.

The only unholy part of Jesus's entire life was his death. When he hung upon the cross, he was covered for an instant by our unholiness. Did you ever wonder why he cried, "My God, my God, why have you forsaken me?" For our sake, Jesus was forsaken.

God protects his holiness. Wrath—righteous anger toward that which will destroy—and judgment await those who have not taken God's character seriously. Your sin, my sin, and the sins of all people for all time were put on Jesus. He became sin for us, and the Father turned away. Our offense against a holy God required a holy settlement we could never pay. What followed was an unholy death because you and I mattered so much that he was willing to pay for us. God will not compromise his holiness, but through Christ he satisfied it. He allowed his Son to be covered by our sin and then he covered our sin with sacrificial blood—all so you and I, though unholy, could be made capable of having a relationship with a holy God.

Revealed through His Church

There's a final way that God reveals his holiness—through his church gathered and his church scattered. First Corinthians 3:16 says, "Do you not know that you are a temple of God and that the Spirit of God dwells in you?" (NASB). The "you" in this verse is plural, speaking of the church gathered. A group of believers gathered for worship are the temple of God and the Spirit of God dwells within them.

The next verse includes a strong warning. "If any man destroys the temple of God, God will destroy him, for the temple of God is holy, and that is what you are" (1 Cor. 3:17 NASB). God's temple, his people, are a holy place that he has pledged to protect. Those who harm the church will come to harm. But those who are still lost in the world ought to be able to walk into any gathering of believers and sense the presence, the power, and the holiness of God, because he dwells among his people.

God's holiness remains even when we aren't gathered together. Another verse in the same book says, "Do you not know that your body is a temple of the Holy Spirit who is in you, whom you have from God, and that you are not your own? For you have been bought with a price: therefore glorify God in your body" (1 Cor. 6:19–20 NASB). Here the "you" is singular each time, not plural. God's holiness dwells in you and me at the same time, even when we are apart. When a believer in Christ goes to work, stays at home, plays softball, is online, or is out shopping, the Spirit of the living God dwells inside.

How Do We Respond to God's Holiness?

Before we can think seriously about what it means for us to respond to God's holiness, we must overcome two obvious obstacles. First, if God is so holy that he can't even gaze at sin, how can sinful people like us have a relationship with him? The truth is, we often feel like Isaiah long before we step into God's presence—we instinctively know that seeing God means trouble for us. As the Bible puts it, we love darkness rather than light. We suspect that seeing God clearly means he will see us clearly, and that can't be good for us. But we're wrong.

The answer that overcomes the first obstacle between us and God's holiness is the cross of Christ. The arrangements have already been made for you to approach the God who is holy. A very costly permission has been paid for in full by Jesus and handed to you freely, with your name already engraved. When Jesus died upon the cross, your sin was covered. You now have a priceless, all-access pass into the holy presence. You can accept that gift and become a part of his family, or you can reject that gift and face an eternity outside of God's holiness, lost in your sin. If you have already accepted that gift, you will face an eternity of exciting discoveries about yourself and about this holy God.

When believers start getting excited about exploring God's holiness, another obstacle almost immediately comes into the picture. If trusting in Christ's work on the cross blocked out our sin before God and we are holy in his sight, why do we keep on sinning? God is holy and never sins; we are called saints (holy) and we sin all the time. How can this be?

Before I respond to the question, let me urge you to consult some resources that will give you much more complete answers than we have space for here. J. I. Packer's book *Knowing God* will be of great help to you. I've also written a book titled *The Miracle of Life Change* that details this process as it's spelled out in Ephesians 4.

Briefly, there are three aspects of holiness as we experience it.

Justification

The moment you understand that God is holy and you have sinned, you turn from your sin, trust in Christ's work on the cross to pay for your sin, and pray to receive Christ. You are immediately *justified*. That's a positional holiness—you have been declared holy by virtue of your position in Christ. God clicks "delete" and the list of all your sins on the screen vanishes into cyberspace. Then he clicks "paste" and the righteousness of Christ fills the column under your name. Whenever God opens your file, he finds the righteousness of his Son credited to you.

Sanctification

But if you're like me, you woke up on Monday morning and realized that you still had the same struggles with temptation. That's where the second aspect of holiness—practical holiness, or *sanctification*—comes in. Once you've put your trust in Christ, the Spirit of God does dwell in you, but now you face a battle. You have enemies—your own tendencies and habits, the world, your lack of biblical knowledge, your lack of fellowship with other believers, and the devil himself. God will use his Scriptures, the spirit dwelling inside you, and relationships with other believers to help you grow in the real knowledge of Christ. Over time, you'll become more like him. It's a process. It can only be measured in longer lengths of time. On a month-by-month or year-by-year basis, how do you and I track the development of holiness in our lives? It's an up-and-down journey, and the point of the process is progress (1 Tim. 4:15).

Glorification

The third aspect of holiness is permanent. You and I are going to die, or the Lord is going to return, and the moment you meet him the process of holiness will be suddenly over. This moment is called *glorification*—you'll be permanently holy. It's a done deal. If you confuse these three aspects of holiness, you can get very frustrated.

Essentials for Holiness

Even though there are obstacles to our practice of holiness, we have everything we need to proceed. There are things that are essential for you to understand in order to grow in holiness:

- It's a commitment we make.

- It's a way that we think.

- It's a command we obey.

- It's an attitude we develop.

These four responses cover the process we're involved in from the moment we receive Christ until the moment he receives us in heaven and our growth is complete. As you read them, remember that God has a lot at stake in your life. Be willing to sense his direction. The agenda of the eternal God of the universe is to display through you individually and all of his people collectively his own character for this world to see.

It's a commitment we make.

We don't slide into a holy life. Holiness doesn't fit on a list of optional spiritual features in our lives as Christians. Hebrews 12:14 says, "Make every effort to live in peace with all men and to be holy; without holiness no one will see the Lord." Make every effort—that sounds like commitment. This verse leads us to some compelling questions: Are you making every effort to be at peace with everyone and to live a holy life? Do you give the same kind of effort to living a holy life as being a good parent, a good marriage partner, or a good friend? Are you giving the same effort to being a holy Christian as you are to earning a living?

If you can't answer yes to those questions, I encourage you to pray a commitment prayer today and say, "Lord, I'm going to commit to deal with anything and everything that causes me to be less than pure and pleasing in your sight. I'm going to be a believer who reflects your holiness in my life."

It's a way that we think.

A radical, holy, winsome life affects your brain. As you read the following passage, note all the words that have to do with what goes into your mind and your thinking:

> So I tell you this, and insist on it in the Lord, that you must no longer live as the Gentiles do, in the futility of their *thinking*. They are darkened in their *understanding* and separated from the life of God because of the *ignorance* that is in them due to the hardening of their hearts. Having lost all sensitivity, they have given themselves over to sensuality so as to indulge in every kind of impurity, with a continual lust for more.

> You, however, did not come to *know* Christ that way. Surely you heard of him and were *taught* in him in accordance with the truth that is in Jesus. You were *taught*, with regard to your former way of life, to put off your old self, which is being corrupted by its deceitful desires; to be

made new in the attitude of your *minds*; and to put on the new self, created to be like God in true righteousness and holiness. (Eph. 4:17–24,
emphasis added)

Responding to God's holiness requires a new way of thinking. A key
issue in your growth is what happens in your brain. What do you allow
into your brain through your eyes and ears, or through the sites you visit,
shows you watch, books you read, or music you listen to? What is your
brain hungry for that you are withholding? How much of God's Word
are you feeding your mind? The verses spell out in black and white the
choices we make that lead toward holiness or away from it. What we
devote our minds to makes all the difference.

It's a command we obey.

Earlier, I mentioned Peter's words to those he called obedient children.
Think through them slowly. "As obedient children, do not conform to
the evil desires you had when you lived in ignorance. But just as he who
called you is holy, so be holy in all you do; for it is written: 'Be holy,
because I am holy'" (1 Pet. 1:14–16).

"Just as he who called you is holy" sets up the compelling standard.
"Be holy" is the command. "In all you do" is the command's stunning
scope. That's why the details in life are secondary to the core motivation. We can't be selectively holy. We can't choose holiness in one area
in exchange for accepting evil in another. This is about understanding
that God is other, different, and distinct. He expects us to be other,
different, and distinct also. This is about living in humble recognition
of the privilege we have to be called the children of such a God. This
is about telling him, without reservation, "God, you have my permission to do whatever you need to do in my life to make me holy." He

didn't spare his own Son, so why would he hold back from answering a prayer like that?

There's a world out there that is dying. We have mass shootings, children are trafficked, families are crumbling, people are shacking up to avoid marriage, babies are aborted, people are shooting up and contracting diseases—all ultimately because they haven't heard compelling reasons or witnessed compelling examples not to! Christians are not providing enough salt of preservation or light of exposure in a winsome, compassionate way.

The two greatest challenges for purity in the early church and in the church today involve the areas of sexuality and money. The writer of Hebrews, in addressing Christians falling away from the truth, writes, "Marriage should be honored by all, and the marriage bed kept pure, for God will judge the adulterer and all the sexually immoral. Keep your lives free from the love of money and be content with what you have, because God has said, 'Never will I leave you; never will I forsake you'" (Heb. 13:4–5).

The words about the marriage bed being "kept pure" literally mean "kept holy." God will judge adulterers because they are violating his holy character and destroying the very institution designed to reflect the beauty and the purity of the bride of Christ.

We should not be surprised at the lack of power and impact of most believers and churches today when cohabitation, unbiblical divorce, casual sex, and consumption of pornography has become commonplace among God's people; one survey found that 68 percent of Christian men and 50 percent of Christian pastors visit porn sites weekly.[2]

Sex may be the symptom, but the core issue behind immoral sexual practice is idolatry. Sex is driven by lust and is self-focused. It uses people and perverts God's design for love and intimacy that is rooted in trust and dependency upon God himself. Spiritual growth and spiritual impact require sexual purity.

The verses above also confront materialism, a modern epidemic in our culture. Verse five tells us the problem (love of money) and the solution (be content). Sexual sin may grab the headlines, but materialism is the sacred cow in the church. I find no greater indictment of the condition of our hearts than our financial practice. Statistics show that only 5 percent of folks who claim to be committed believers give a tithe (10 percent or more) of their annual income.[3] Jesus clearly taught us that our hearts always follow our treasure, and that we cannot serve both God and money.

I don't mean to sound harsh, but the reality of our behavior and our unholiness has brought incredible pain and dysfunction to our lives and families while simultaneously hindering our testimony and the gospel. We are the wealthiest nation in the world and yet we cannot support our own missionaries who go unfunded. While they wait and God's kingdom is hindered, we have our toys, our clothes, our jewelry, our second and third homes, and we seem oblivious to God's call and agenda. Our lives are hurried and busy with work, money, sports, and the pursuit of the American dream.

We blame Hollywood, the media, video games, terrible people, or the educational system, but if Christians lived like Christians, things would be remarkably different. If all forty million Americans who claim the name of Jesus took God's holiness seriously, the entire country would be transformed in ten years. Remember that the way we act as believers and as a church states clearly what we actually think about God. What are our actions and words telling the world about who God is?

We know the problem, and it's mostly us. But we're under command to stop, turn around, and pursue holiness. We will have to develop a whole new attitude.

It's an attitude we develop.

"To fear the LORD is to hate evil; I hate pride and arrogance, evil behavior and perverse speech" (Prov. 8:13).

The attitude of holiness is not a haughty, holier-than-thou treatment of others. It is an uncompromising, gut-level rejection of evil behavior. Holiness is definitely an unpopular attitude in a time of tolerance, extreme individuality, and rampant immorality. Although the phrase, "Do not be unequally yoked together with unbelievers" (2 Cor. 6:14 NKJV) is most often quoted in discussions about marriages between believers and unbelievers, the context includes all of life. It's impossible for light and darkness to fellowship with each other; our interaction with the world *will* affect our spiritual well-being. Paul shows many contrasts between Christ and Belial, believers and unbelievers, the temple of God and idols—all intended to impress upon us the importance of holiness. He underscores the application by reminding us that the temple of God is not a building:

> What agreement is there between the temple of God and idols?
>> For we are the temple of the living God. . . .
> "Therefore come out from them
>> and be separate,
>> says the Lord.
> Touch no unclean thing,
>> and I will receive you.
> I will be a Father to you,

and you will be my sons and daughters,
says the Lord Almighty." (2 Cor. 6:16–18)

The practical action can be found in the first verse of the next chapter. "Since we have these promises, dear friends, let us purify ourselves from everything that contaminates body and spirit, perfecting holiness out of reverence for God" (2 Cor. 7:1). The goal is to become separate. We are to be *in* the world but not *of* it. This command is not a call to offend other people by making them feel inferior; it is a call to pursue personal holiness out of respect for the One who has done so much for us.

I spent the first years of my Christian life trying to stay as close to sin as possible without falling in. My commitment was halfhearted, my thinking hadn't changed, I wasn't listening to the Spirit, and my attitude was still dominated by my previous life. God's holiness wasn't even on my radar screen. Like many today, I was too busy compromising. The result was frustration and guilt within, while my life exhibited an embarrassing contradiction without. The turning point for me came when I began to view evil the same way God does.

If you want to be holy, you must develop an attitude that promotes holiness. Namely: hate evil, pursue God with all your heart, and if you're in doubt, don't. Embrace Christ and his purity while saying, "God, I don't want to waste my time weighing the promises of sin against your promises. I know your way of holiness is far better as a way of living and offers a far better destination."

God longs for you to see his holiness and to want it mirrored in your life. Your desires for intimacy, love, fulfillment, and satisfaction are only truly fulfilled in his way and in his time. The best things in life are wrapped in God's holiness.

My Experience with the Holiness of God

Andy had a secret. It was a secret he had kept hidden for over twenty years. His secret started as a young preteen scanning the pages of the Sears catalog. He later graduated to magazines in his teen and college years.

Andy trusted Christ in his late teens and saw nearly every area of his life miraculously transformed in the next fifteen years; that is, every area except his little secret. Despite becoming a leader in college ministry and later becoming a devoted father and deacon in the church, Andy's secret continued and progressed to adult bookstores and late-night internet exploring. The guilt and the double life brought such internal conflict and shame that Andy thought he would explode. He tried everything. He prayed. He memorized Scripture. He fasted. He begged God for deliverance. He swore multiple times with absolute sincerity that he would break this addiction and live a holy life before God. He failed repeatedly.

Then one day in desperation, Andy traveled to another city and, for the first time, shared his secret with a group of men who understood. That critical step was the beginning of Andy's restoration to his God, his wife, his friends, and to himself.

When darkness is brought into the light, it loses its power. At the church I pastored in California, Andy shared about his painful journey of sexual addiction to pornography and about God's deliverance. In humility and with great discretion, Andy called our men to come "into the light," to destroy the power of the secret, and to walk in holiness together—in the strength of genuine community.

We launched a number of small groups for men with sexual addictions the very next week. We watched God do the miraculous. We learned that the highway to holiness is never traveled alone. We need each other. We must confess our sins to one another so that we may be healed (see James 5:16).

So what's your secret? Where are you struggling? Whom could you tell in order to break the power of the secret and let God's light expose, cleanse, and restore you for his glory?

God deeply loves you and it is in holiness that we find wholeness and peace. I encourage you to take a bold step of honesty. Ask God to reveal any unclean or unholy issue in your life. Walk in the light that you might be free from guilt and shame.

Live It Out—B.I.O.

"Bio" is a word that is synonymous with "life." Found in those three simple letters, B.I.O. is the key to helping you become the person God wants you to be.

- **B** *Come BEFORE God daily.* Meet with him personally through his Word and prayer to enjoy his presence, receive his direction, and follow his will.

- **I** *Do Life IN COMMUNITY weekly.* Structure your week to personally connect in safe relationships that provide love, support, transparency, challenge, and accountability.

- **O** *ON MISSION 24/7.* Cultivate a mindset to "live out" Jesus's love for others through acts of sacrifice and service at home, work, play, and church.

Come BEFORE God

- Write the following definition on a notecard, smartphone, or tablet and place it where you will read it when you get up in the morning and when you go to bed. Don't try to memorize it. Simply read it in a spirit of prayer and let the reality of God's holiness gently pour over your soul.

> We know nothing like the divine holiness. It stands apart, unique, unapproachable, incomprehensible and unattainable. The natural man is blind to it. He may fear God's power and admire His wisdom, but His holiness he cannot even imagine. Only the Spirit of the Holy One can impart to the human spirit the knowledge of the holy.[4]

> A. W. Tozer

- Near the definition, write 1 Peter 1:14–16 and meditate on that command. Each time you read it, begin by asking, "How can I reflect God's character today?"

> Do not be conformed to the former lusts which were yours in your ignorance, but like the Holy One who called you, be holy yourselves also in all your behavior; because it is written, "YOU SHALL BE HOLY, FOR I AM HOLY." (1 Pet. 1:14–16 NASB)

- Join me in making the following prayer your own for the next seven days:

> *O Lord God, holy and pure, awesome in majesty, as I consider your perfection, grant that I might*
>
> - *commit to holy ways,*
>
> - *think holy thoughts,*

- *live in holy obedience, and*

- *reject evil with a holy attitude.*

Let me hear the tender conviction of your Spirit and help me remember that you are jealous for your holiness. Because of your love, you see the pain our sin will bring us, and you long to rescue us. So that your name may never be profaned in my life, please do whatever you need to do to make me holy. In Jesus's name, Amen.

Do Life IN Community

- Read Galatians 5:16–17.

So I say, live by the Spirit, and you will not gratify the desires of the sinful nature. For the sinful nature desires what is contrary to the Spirit, and the Spirit what is contrary to the sinful nature. They are in conflict with each other, so that you do not do what you want.

- What can you learn from this passage about the pursuit of holiness?

- According to Galatians 5, these are the results from following:

  - *the desires of the sinful nature*: sexual immorality, impurity, lustful pleasures, idolatry, sorcery, hostility, quarreling, jealousy, outbursts of anger, selfish ambition, division, envy, drunkenness, and wild parties.

  - *the desires of the Spirit:* love, joy, peace, patience, kindness, goodness, faithfulness, gentleness, and self-control.

- Which results do you see in your life? Are the results evidence of the Spirit at work? The sinful nature? Both?

- It is clear that the desires of the Spirit and the desires of the sinful nature are always in conflict with each other. Who can help encourage and support you as you commit to the Spirit's work in your life? Who can you help and encourage?

Be ON Mission

- Is there an area in your life that has been compromising or hurting your testimony with unbelievers? Spend some time praying and reflecting on this question. Then, respond obediently to whatever God reveals to you.

7

THE WISDOM OF GOD

Oh, the depth of the riches both of the wisdom and knowledge of God! How unsearchable are His judgments and unfathomable His ways!

Romans 11:33 NASB

I was nearing the end of my third year of seminary. To make ends meet, I'd been working full-time while taking a full load of classes. My salary came from commissions, and the marketplace had suddenly dried up. Home life was nonstop action with an eighteen-month-old baby and rambunctious twin boys. Beyond that, Theresa and I were involved in a flourishing college ministry, which, along with success, produced more and more stress. I was at the end of my emotional rope.

For three years I had gotten less than five hours of sleep each night. I was discouraged, tired, and broke. I didn't know how we were going to pay the bills, and I was seriously contemplating calling it quits. "If this is what you get when you follow Christ with all your heart," I thought, "maybe it's time to check out of the Christian life—at least the ministry part of it."

That year I had a theology class in which the professor spoke in very clear, precise statements. I often didn't write down his words because they had a way of sticking in my brain immediately. I can still picture this very thin man with wire-rimmed glasses, his hands neatly clasped behind his back, clearing his throat and saying, "Students, the wisdom of God tells us that God will bring about the best possible results, by the best possible means, for the most possible people, for the longest possible time." He didn't raise his voice or change his tone, but the words entered my ears in bold type. They instantly challenged the chaos of my life. I ran his statement through my mind, mixing it with the crises we were facing. I knew immediately that something had to be wrong either with these words or with my perspective. They couldn't both be true.

> **"Students, the wisdom of God tells us that God will bring about the best possible results, by the best possible means, for the most possible people, for the longest possible time."**

I remember wondering what it would be like if I actually believed my professor's statement. I would have to conclude that God was sovereignly allowing that set of circumstances to do something in me, through me, in my relationships, in my marriage, in my work, and in my worship that could not be accomplished any other way. As far as I knew, I was walking in obedience to him. That meant that what I was experiencing in those circumstances was the best possible means happening in the best possible way to produce the best possible results in my life.

"Which also means," I thought, "if there were a better way to do it, then I would be experiencing those other circumstances instead of these. If there were a kinder, faster, more expedient, or gentler way, God would be using it."

It was a hard truth to swallow. The circumstances I was in, if God is all-wise, were exactly what I needed for that period in my life. He didn't miss, not even by a couple degrees. I was in the center of his will and the discomfort and exhaustion was from the hand of a loving Father who had my highest good in mind.

So I began to think about my circumstances that way. I didn't quit school. And though my circumstances didn't change, I did. My view of God got clearer, and my faith grew stronger.

Those changes in perspective led me to a decision I would never have contemplated otherwise. While finishing school, I accepted a position at Country Bible Church in the rural community of Kaufman, Texas. The prospects of success and security didn't point in that direction, but God's Spirit did. It didn't look like a place that could supply what I *thought* we needed, but it turned out to be the place where God supplied what we *really* needed. Among the folks at that church, God taught me how to be a pastor. He prepared me for my next several steps in ministry.

Isn't it amazing how God works? Imagine, if you will, what a difference it would make in life's most difficult times if you and I could believe that God is all-wise. What difference would it make if you firmly believed that the problem in your life that is most pressing and difficult—the one you don't understand, that you chafe against, that makes you feel overwhelmed and ready to give up—was allowed or orchestrated by an all-wise, loving Father? What if *everything* in your life was part of a wise plan? Can you imagine what would happen to your anxiety level and your emotions? Can you fathom what a difference it would make if you were absolutely convinced that a sovereign, good, loving God is producing the best possible results in your life by the best possible means—not his Plan B or C, but the Plan A designed specifically for you?

I will tell you what difference it would make. The wisdom of God properly understood will revolutionize your life. It has revolutionized mine. From that point of desperation on, I have looked at circumstances differently and have experienced progressive spiritual growth. I discovered this unavoidable truth: *until we grasp what it means that God is all-wise, we will never be able to trust and rest in his wise plan for our lives.*

Defining God's Wisdom

The very mention of *wisdom* brings up a lot of stereotypes and misunderstandings. Certain pictures come into our mind, and most of them have to do with how we think wise people look rather than what they do. But wisdom has nothing to do with white hair or beard length. Even children—especially children who know God's Word—can often utter astonishing wisdom.

Wisdom refers to the way someone uses knowledge and experience. Dictionaries describe it as the ability to judge rightly and then follow the soundest course of action. In other words, wise people see the big picture and make good decisions. How? It's based on knowledge, experience, and understanding. Wisdom includes knowing, showing, being, and doing. Wisdom, Proverbs tells us, is rooted in fearing God, the ultimate source of wisdom.

The theme verse for this chapter, Romans 11:33, praises the wisdom of God. Paul breaks into a song that expresses a wonderful frustration we

will always have—we will never figure out God's wisdom. God's decisions (judgments) are "unsearchable," which means we can't examine
or question them with any hope of satisfaction. God's paths are beyond
our ability to trace. We can't follow what he is doing without getting
lost and confused. But we can trust. I love Tozer's practical insight
concerning God's wisdom:

> **Quick Definition**
>
> To believe actively that our Heavenly Father constantly spreads
> around us providential circumstances that work for our present
> good and our everlasting well-being brings to the soul a veritable
> benediction. Most of us go through life praying a little, planning a
> little, jockeying for position, hoping but never being quite certain of
> anything, and always secretly afraid that we will miss the way. This
> is a tragic waste of truth and never gives rest to the heart.
>
> There is a better way. It is to repudiate our own wisdom and take
> instead the infinite wisdom of God. Our insistence upon seeing
> ahead is natural enough, but it is a real hindrance to our spiritual
> progress. God has charged Himself with full responsibility for our
> eternal happiness and stands ready to take over the management
> of our lives the moment we turn in faith to Him.[1]

Read that last sentence again. God has staked his reputation on taking
care of us. How often do we take him at his word in the way we live?
If this is really true, if it has that much power, if the light would go on
from our head down to our heart, what a difference that would make!
When we face illnesses that won't go away, biopsy reports that don't
make sense, relationships that just don't seem to get right no matter
what, wouldn't it be a relief to rest and trust that an all-wise God is
sovereignly in control and working for my good?

Yes it would, if you and I could but remember that God's wisdom has a larger scope than we will ever imagine. As Tozer puts it, "[Wisdom] sees the end from the beginning, so there can be no guess or conjecture. Wisdom sees everything in focus, each in proper relation to all, and thus is able to work toward predestined goals, with flawless precision."[2]

Let me give an illustration. Suppose a man has a job as a railroad operator, controlling train traffic by switching tracks. Day after day, he sits in a little booth high above the railway yard, watching carefully as speeding trains rumble through. They depend on him to prevent accidents.

One day, the operator's five-year-old boy comes to visit his father from their nearby home. Seeing Dad up in the control booth, he runs shouting and waving across the railroad tracks. Just as his dad notices him, he trips and gets his foot caught between a switching track. He's stuck.

The man leaps to his feet to help his boy, but a piercing whistle gets his attention. He looks to the left in horror and sees a speeding train a few hundred yards away. Even if it braked immediately, it wouldn't stop in time.

The father is forced to make a split-second decision. He can't reach the boy in time. He can shift the tracks and derail the train, killing many of the people on board while saving his son. Or he can allow the passengers to continue safely, oblivious to the tragedy outside as the operator watches his son die on the tracks.

What's the wisest choice in that terrible moment? Not "what's the best choice," not "what's the most personal choice," and not even "what choice do I want to make," but what's the *wisest* choice? What would bring the best possible result for the most possible people? Most of us would probably say that the hardest but wisest decision would be to let the son be killed and save all the people. Maybe so. I would suggest that we just don't know.

What if that son was the next Billy Graham? What if forty-three people died on the train, but the boy's ministry helped millions and millions of people spend eternity in heaven? Or what if the next great evangelist was on the train? Or what if the cure for cancer was on the train? The "what ifs" never end, but you and I will never have that much knowledge to juggle in decision making. The only person who could make the wisest decision in this father's horrible dilemma is the One who knows all things about all people, and how they will impact one another each moment and forever.

Our lives are like pebbles dropped into the lake of world history, and the ripples impact countless other people, generation after generation. It would take an incomprehensibly wise person to keep track of it all. The jumble of decisions, actions, and events that affect others is mind-boggling. Even the small part that we do see makes us think sometimes that the world is absolute chaos. But controlling his creation is like doing simple math for God. In one instant, he sees all relationships, all impact, all costs, all implications, and how it all fits into his wise plan in a fallen world.

And because you are his child, God orchestrates or allows only the best possible results, by the best possible means, to accomplish the highest possible purpose, for the longest time, for the most people in and around your life. Only God can make the wisest choice.

We get caught up in thinking we know what's wisest because we get little windows into truth and life. We jump to conclusions about what must be done. Sometimes we're right and sometimes we're completely wrong. Unfortunately, we often put our hands on our hips and demand, "Hey, God, what about this situation? What about that problem? What about that person? If you had only done this or prevented that, everything would be so much better!" Our arrogance is stunning. Every time I catch myself beginning to question God's judgment, I visit the last few chapters of the book of Job, where God responds to questions about his wisdom. He doesn't argue or defend himself. He simply points out that in the grand scope of things, we know nothing. When it comes to divine wisdom, we haven't been there and we haven't done that.

I hate to admit it, but I know how easy it is for us to act as if we are wiser than God. We need to continually see ourselves in our proper place as creatures before our Creator. Tozer helps us move from humility to worship:

> All God's acts are done in perfect wisdom, first for His own glory, and then for the highest good of the greatest number for the longest time. All His acts are as pure as they are wise, and as good as they are wise and pure. Not only could His acts not be better done: a better way to do them could not be imagined.[3]

It takes time and repeated lessons to bring us to the place where we consistently treat God's wisdom with awe and respect. It's easier for us to define God's wisdom than to willingly live under it. Part of our training will include reviewing the ways God has revealed and continues to reveal his mind to us. That will help us when we can't immediately discern his wisdom in our surroundings or circumstances.

How Has God Revealed His Wisdom to Us?

We've learned the definition of wisdom: it's the attribute of God whereby he will produce the best possible results by the best possible means. But how do we know? What evidence has he given us that we can trust his invisible hand even in our darkest moments?

Through Creation

First, God has revealed his wisdom to us through creation. If you ponder the workings of creation, you will never cease to be amazed. From the inner workings of the subatomic universe to the vast reaches of space, this astounding creation functions like a finely tuned system. In fact, one of the things that amazes me is how much faith it takes to conclude that all of this occurred by accident. The cosmos displays an obvious design for all to see. The more we understand that behind every effect there is a cause, the more we will appreciate the greatness and the wisdom of the first cause, namely God.

God's creation talks to us. "The heavens declare the glory of God; the skies proclaim the work of his hands. Day after day they pour forth speech; night after night they display knowledge" (Ps. 19:1). How well are we listening? The heavens put on a show; are we watching? The rest of that psalm describes the wisdom of God's creation and his law. Psalm 104:24 makes the connection between wisdom and creation clear: "How many are your works, O LORD! In wisdom you made them all; the earth is full of your creatures."

Our ecosystem displays all the signs of divine planning. We are only beginning to understand the intricate balance that we disturb with a little garbage here and there. The system is amazingly resilient— hundreds of years of old-growth forest can be incinerated in hours by a careless spark; yet weeks later, the first signs of renewed life sprout through the charred earth. But the world is also surprisingly precarious. If the tilt of the earth were off by just a fraction of a degree, some of us would be burning up while others would stay in a deep freeze.

A look at the planetary system and galaxies proves the magnificence of God's work. My father was a science teacher, and he often took us out to gaze at stars through his telescope. "You know, you don't find many astronomers who are atheists," he would tell us. "You just don't."

We don't have to go that far to contemplate the most wonderful system in creation. Have you ever marveled at the human body? What amazing testaments to creative genius and wisdom! We are, in the psalmist's words, "wonderfully complex" organisms. The balanced and efficient ways our bodily systems operate is incomprehensible.

The body's ability to repair itself is one of the most awe-inspiring aspects of God's wisdom. Imagine someone who had never seen blood accidentally cutting his arm. He might be horrified, but that's not a big deal to us. We would casually say, "Oh, don't worry, it miraculously heals itself." Did you know that a broken bone—even a compound fracture—will heal in such a way that it begins to fill in bone on the side where it is needed the most? How does the body know to do that? The DNA inside a single cell could stretch for miles, and somehow all your cells know exactly what to do at which times. And then the brain—our best computers don't even come close!

I had a kinesiology teacher in graduate school who was not a believer. Yet, she would hold up a skeleton and talk about the human form and system as if she were a royal priestess of the body. She would look at it in complete awe because she just couldn't fathom how wonderfully it was made and how effectively it worked. Even though she missed obvious glimpses of the Creator, she was entranced by the creation. It's an amazing design.

Through Providence

God also reveals his wisdom through divine providence. In theological language, that's the term used to describe how God works all things together for good. He provides what is needed for his purposes. "The LORD foils the plans of the nations; he thwarts the purposes of the peoples," says Psalm 33:10–11. "But the plans of the LORD stand firm forever, the purposes of his heart through all generations." The ebb and flow of history may appear out of control or random at times, but God is the final arbiter of success and failure. This theme is reiterated in the New Testament by Paul: "And we know that in all things God works for the good of those who love him, who have been called according to his purpose" (Rom. 8:28).

History is littered with powerful nations that have said they were going to dominate the world. Some have even appeared to succeed for a while. The Persians, Greeks, Romans, and many more all the way up to the Nazis are empires that rose and fell. God foiled their plans. Meanwhile, like a thin thread that runs through history, a chosen people called Israel stubbornly remain on the world stage. God has pledged himself to their preservation. By his providence, they survive. Scattered, persecuted, and subjected to blatant genocide, Israel still thrives. Twenty centuries of distance from the Promised Land was not long enough to break the ties. And in 1948 they again became a recognized nation and the center of world attention.

The God who has a purpose for nations also has a purpose for people. I love hearing people tell stories about God's wisdom in their lives. Something terrible happens in one person's life, yet afterward she realizes she never would have met her husband if the event hadn't happened. Others take a "wrong" turn and find a job. I heard someone tell how he shattered a leg, which caused him to be stuck in the hospital for days. During the downtime, he read a book that led him to Christ.

God apparently doesn't hesitate to let you break your leg (or worse) if it will allow you to meet him.

I've seen God's providence many times. I shared at the beginning of this chapter how I was ready to cash the whole Christian life in. God shut down my job and I got discouraged and desperate. At first, I just needed to put bread on the table. A little group of thirty-five people in a town that didn't even have a stoplight invited me to be their pastor. Theresa and I sat in a Chinese restaurant talking about whether this was God's will. "Please don't take me there," she said through tears of apprehension.

"Honey, I believe this is God's will for our life," I told her. She nodded her head and we both cried some more. We couldn't feel God's providence at the moment, but we learned. Today I know that some of the greatest people on the face of the earth are in Kaufman, Texas. My family and I needed what God ordained for them to give us, and apparently in some measure they needed what God ordained for us to give them. We could easily have said we didn't think it was wise to go there at that point in our lives, and we would have been wrong. In his wisdom, God had a better plan.

Through Redemption

God also reveals his wisdom through the plan of redemption. The word *redemption* literally means "to buy back." It also refers to the wise process God used to reestablish a relationship with that part of creation that sold itself into slavery to sin—you and me.

Yet from the foundations of the earth, God purposed in his wisdom to redeem us for himself. Our own rebellious sin had to be judged because he is holy. His love wanted restoration. His justice demanded a settlement.

His grace provided the willingness. And God's wisdom—taking all other attributes into account—devised the plan. Our redemption begins and ends with God's wisdom.

Sin and rebellion against the perfect, holy God required absolute satisfaction. There had to be a perfect sacrifice. Jesus, God in the flesh, died on the cross with his blood as the redemption payment for us. He described the transaction this way: "For even the Son of Man did not come to be served, but to serve, and to give his life as a ransom for many" (Mark 10.45).

Here's the rest of the story. God's wisdom caught even the spiritual world off guard. Satan and the demonic angels saw the Son of God come, and they probably thought it was a foolish plan, doomed to failure. A teenage girl in a stable? A carpenter's boy? Not a chance.

They were scoffing and scheming while Jesus was growing up like a typical kid. He passed through temptation in the wilderness, chose his disciples, and began his ministry. And Jesus didn't exactly pick out the Einsteins of the world to be his closest associates. He chose a motley crew of fishermen, liars, thieves, a zealot, and an outcast.

Satan must have been thinking, "We're going to crush him." The evil scheme worked flawlessly, much to the delight of the forces of evil. They laughed while Jesus hung on the cross. "We trumped up charges, we killed the Christ, and now we're going to win it all."

That's creature wisdom. In the wisdom of God, it's better that one might die so that all others might live forever, so Jesus voluntarily paid that price. From the perspective of creature wisdom, he failed miserably. His enemies seriously underestimated what he meant when he cried, "It is finished!" from the cross. They thought *he* was finished. They were wrong.

Jesus went into the earth for three days. During that time he proclaimed victory over his enemies, he conquered sin, he conquered death, and he declared victory. Colossians 2:15 says he disarmed and embarrassed the devil. Christ turned the tables on the opposition and brought about redemption precisely as planned by the wisdom of God.

Through Christ, His Son

The ultimate picture of God's wisdom is Christ himself. First Corinthians 1:30 says, "It is because of him that you are in Christ Jesus, who has become for us wisdom from God—that is, our righteousness, holiness and redemption." Christ is the wisdom of God. If you want to understand how life ought to work, get rightly connected to Christ and follow him, and you will be in the heart of God's wisdom.

Not only will Christ affect you internally, his wisdom will overflow into people. "But the wisdom that comes from heaven is first of all pure; then peace-loving, considerate, submissive, full of mercy and good fruit, impartial and sincere" (James 3:17). When you begin to live out this wisdom, it produces awesome relationships, glory to God, and peace and well-being to you. So how can we tap into this supernatural wisdom for living?

How Do We Respond to the Wisdom of God?

When God allows, brings, or orchestrates circumstances in our lives—no matter how many relationships or other influences, factors, and decisions are involved—he knows all things about all people, actual and possible. God tracks the implications of all that happens in you, through you, around you and to everyone, forever. We think that's not possible, but what's not possible for us is child's play for God.

Unfortunately, I can know all about God's wisdom but fail to benefit from it. I can know he's revealed it in creation, in providence, in redemption, and in Christ, but I still face the question: How does it work for me on Monday morning?

How does it work when my wife and I are not getting along? How does it work when I'm in a financial crisis? How does it work when I feel overwhelmed, overloaded, ashamed, and ready to give up? How do you and I respond to everything God allows into our lives? The answer to those questions is deceptively simple: we need to learn to live wisely. God advises us, "Be very careful, then, how you live— not as unwise but as wise, making the most of every opportunity, because the days are evil. Therefore do not be foolish, but understand what the Lord's will is" (Eph. 5:15–17).

Living wisely means living in accordance with God's Word. If we are not cooperating—if we are not aligned with God, guided by his Word, instructed by his Spirit, in the community of his people—then we will be living an unwise life. If you are not walking in God's wise path, consider the hardships you're experiencing as guardrails. God set them up to steer you back to him. Hitting those guardrails hurts! Yet God says, "Would you please pick up this candle I've provided for you so I could give you clear direction about how to live my way in your marriage, in your singleness, with your kids, with your money, and in your decision making."

That candle is God's Word—it's a lamp to our feet and a light to our path (Ps. 119:105).

When you do pick up God's candle (his Word), you will discover at least four prerequisites to wise living:

1. Wise living begins with reverence for God.

"The fear of the LORD is the beginning of wisdom, and knowledge of the Holy One is understanding" (Prov. 9:10). The fear of the Lord is basically this: you personally recognize that he's the Creator, Master, CEO of the universe, he's holy, and he's awesome; in response you willfully choose to do life his way and to submit to the authority of his word. This process begins with a very important step of faith. The first, deepest, wisest decision you can make is to receive the salvation God offers freely. To paraphrase missionary Jim Elliot, it's never foolish to exchange the sin-marred life you cannot keep for the eternal life you can never lose. You must ask Christ to be your Savior, a request you cannot seriously make unless you are also ready to say, "I am in great need of you, and I long to live my life in submission to your will."

Without a fear of the Lord there is no wisdom. That's the beginning. If you're outside of Christ, get inside of Christ. Turn from your self and your sin and ask him to come into your life right now. If you are a believer, and you are out of line with God's wisdom—and we've all been there—confess it and make it right. If you simply recognize that your reverence for God is at a low ebb, why not stop right now and do a personal inventory on your priorities? What has caused the leakage in your devotional life? Who or what has come between you and your love for God? Take a moment right now and ask him for help and a restored view of his worthiness and majesty in your heart.

2. Wise living grows by receiving his Word.

Wise living starts with reverence for God, and it grows by receiving his Word. Psalm 119:97–101 describes the process:

Oh, how I love your law!
    I meditate on it all day long.
Your commands make me wiser than my enemies,
    for they are ever with me.
I have more insight than all my teachers,   ·
    for I meditate on your statutes.
I have more understanding than the elders
    for I obey your precepts.
I have kept my feet from every evil path
    so that I might obey your word.

God gives wisdom but he doesn't give it in a vacuum. God's wisdom comes through his Word. As Paul reminded Timothy, "From infancy you have known the holy Scriptures, which are able to make you wise for salvation through faith in Christ Jesus. All Scripture is God-breathed and is useful for teaching, rebuking, correcting and training in righteousness, so that the man of God may be thoroughly equipped for every good work" (2 Tim. 3:15–17). The old apostle was saying, "Timothy, you want the light to be able to follow God in every area of your life? God's Word is the lamp."

I have an aversion to reading instructions. Painful experience has taught me to beware of items that include the notice, "Some assembly required." Crooked barbecue sets and wobbly bicycles testify to my lack of mechanical skill combined with my failure to read the directions.

But when it comes to life I cannot say, "I just don't have time to read the instructions." There's just too much at stake not to pay attention to God's instruction manual.

Spending regular time attentively reading the Scriptures is more important than being online, checking Facebook, watching ESPN, or catching up on any other TV show. It's more significant than the *Wall Street*

Journal, the *New York Times*, or any other newspaper. It's more valuable than your daily diet and exercise. Next to breathing, it's more essential to wise living than anything.

A decision I made over twenty-five years ago helped me develop some discipline in this area. Like many Christians, I struggled the first few years of my Christian life to get into God's Word on a regular basis. So I determined: no Bible, no bread. Until I got in the Word each day, I wouldn't eat. That's not a legalistic requirement, just a personal decision that I needed to make. Since I love to eat, and I usually wake up hungry, I simply expanded my understanding of breakfast to include a daily portion of God's Word. It's been the best habit I ever formed in my life. Until I was feeding on God's wisdom regularly, I wasn't able to take the next step in wise living—asking God for his thoughts on my issues.

3. Wise living requires that we ask for wisdom specifically.

It's one thing to be exposed to God's wisdom by reading his Word; it's another to apply that wisdom in real life. Wise living involves asking God for wisdom specifically. "If any of you lacks wisdom," James tells us, "he should ask God, who gives generously to all without finding fault, and it will be given to him. But when he asks, he must believe and not doubt, because he who doubts is like a wave of the sea, blown and tossed by the wind" (James 1:5–6). As long as we live, we will have moments that expose our lack of wisdom. When we ask God for his, we are turning to the ultimate source. But we are to ask in confidence. James addresses the doubter: "That man should not think he will receive anything from the Lord" (James 1:7). The word *doubt* in these verses literally means "double-minded," someone with a divided mind, a soul with split allegiances. We can't ask God for his wisdom in order to evaluate our options and do whatever we want. That's the kind of double-minded doubting James is referring to. Simply asking for his opinion will not get an answer.

Wise living is decisive dependence on the source of wisdom. We must learn to see every decision as an opportunity to ask God for wisdom. He doesn't mind it at all when we admit, "God, I don't know what to do in this marriage, I don't know what to do with this big decision, I don't know how to handle this kid, I don't know what to do with our finances, I don't know whether I ought to move, and I don't know if I should take this job." But we don't stop there. Here's the single-minded request: "I'm asking you to show me and I'm telling you in advance that I will follow your guidance. I'm signing the bottom of the work order. You fill in the directions above and I will obey them. Whatever you say, I will do."

In those cases, God says, "One hundred percent of the time, I will give you wisdom." He will give wisdom through his Word, he'll give it through wise counsel, and at times he'll give it through circumstances. Just remember that the wisdom you receive will not contradict what God has stated in his Word. The best advice in the world is worthless if it tells you to disregard what God has said.

I have often found that God uses wise counselors and circumstances to give us wisdom. I felt betrayed by a friend, and was not sure how to deal with it. I knew I needed to confront the person, and my "shoot it straight" and "get this over with" mentality was compelling me to go in with guns blazing. I had rehearsed in my mind multiple times what I would say and how I would say it, but each time I opened the Bible I was challenged to get wise counsel and to slow down the process.

Reluctantly, I obeyed and heard the same thing from two wise counselors that the Bible had been repeatedly admonishing me to do—"get the log out of my own eye before I went to remove the speck out of his."

Thanks to these two trusted advisors, I chose to be gracious to the person I was confronting and was able to see that the conflict involved not only his inappropriate behavior but also pride in my own life. Through the Bible's instructions and the counsel of these godly men, God prevented me from opening my mouth and really damaging an important relationship. Why? Because I had been in the Word and I had asked specifically for wisdom.

I spent many of the first ten years of my new life in Christ perplexed about his will and overwhelmed with important decisions. I felt like the weight of the world was upon me and I didn't know what to do. Learning to take God at his word (James 1:5) and pray specifically for wisdom in each situation was a major turning point in my life. The hard part was being willing to do whatever he said, but as I learned to trust, I gradually saw God make his will clearer and easier to understand than I ever imagined.

So how about you? How are you doing in this area of wise living? Are you asking God for wisdom in big and small decisions? When you get it, are you acting on it? If you long to follow God's wise counsel but still find it difficult, perhaps the last prerequisite will help you learn to hear his voice. It's all about trust.

4. Wise living involves learning to trust God completely.

This last step really follows each of the previous ones. Reverence for God involves trusting him. Receiving God's Word on a regular basis will have little impact if we don't trust the truth and the source of that Word. Asking God for wisdom won't mean much if we are double-minded and mistrust his willingness and motives. Ultimately, wise living demands a daily exercise of trust whereby we say in our heart of hearts, "All that comes my way is from the hand of a good and loving God, who, knowing all things actual and possible, is exerting his unlimited power to execute the best possible outcomes, by the best possible means, to fulfill the highest possible purposes for me."

Talking about God's wisdom has to be more than an interesting theological discussion. It is a truth that has the power to transform our perspective and our attitudes even in life's most difficult situations.

To put it another way, what's the most difficult circumstance in your life right now? Think of one that's hard: a persistent problem, a wrecked relationship, a perplexing question, or an agonizing decision. What would it look like if you really believed that God is all-wise and has actually allowed that set of circumstances into your life for his purposes? May I suggest that God's wisdom rightly understood delivers us from self-pity, a "victim mentality," the blame game, and the negative emotions that accompany those unfruitful responses to adversity?

In fact, J. I. Packer captures the impact of grasping God's wisdom in our lives:

> God's almighty wisdom is always active and never fails. All his works of creation and providence and grace display it, and until we can see it in them we just are not seeing them straight. But we cannot recognize God's wisdom unless we know the end for which he is working. . . . God's wisdom is not, and never was, pledged to keep a fallen world happy, or to make ungodliness comfortable. Not even to Christians has he promised a trouble-free life; rather, the reverse. He has other ends in view for life in this world than simply to make it easy for everyone.
>
> What is he after then? What is his goal? What does he aim at? . . . He plans that a great host of humankind should come to love and honor him. His ultimate objective is to bring them to a state in which they please him entirely and praise him adequately, and a state in which he is

all in all to them, and he and they rejoice continually in the knowledge of each other's love—people rejoicing in the saving love of God, set upon them from all eternity, and God rejoicing in the responsive love of people, drawn out of them by grace through the gospel.[4]

We will never be able to trust what God is doing in our lives until we figure out and personalize his ultimate goal. His primary purpose is not to make us happy, healthy, wealthy, and wonderful. He doesn't promise to make our lives easy and guarantee that things go smoothly. Though he is eternally committed to providing the best for his children, that "best" may or may not coincide with what many of us consider "making it" in life. God is good. He is sovereign. And even in a fallen world, we can rest in the assurance that he is actively working to bring about the best possible results by the best possible means, and in the end, to make you and me like his Son, Jesus.

My Personal Experience with the Wisdom of God

The year was 2002. I had prayed, fasted, sought counsel, agonized over the implications, and even been given a promise from God with regard to the next big step in my life. Leave California, leave the church, leave our grown son, leave our home, leave the pastorate, uproot our daughter in the middle of high school, and move to Atlanta to assume the leadership of a Christian organization whose founder had led it for twenty-six years.

I knew what obedience looked like, but it didn't look very wise. I saw the vast potential for spiritual fruitfulness, but felt God's timing could not have been worse.

Days after making the decision, Theresa's mother had complications after surgery that resulted in ninety days in intensive care and her home-going to the Lord. Our California house had termites, our shipped car was damaged in transit in an ice storm, our furniture arrived before the house was ready, our refrigerator was dropped and had to be replaced, the economy bottomed out, and donations were down 38 percent, putting the ministry in financial crisis. My wife was grieving multiple losses simultaneously while undergoing two oral surgeries in the first few months of our arrival in Atlanta.

Where was God? How could this be? *Is this how you reward obedience, Lord? Did you not see this coming, Lord? Or worse, did you see it coming and let it all happen anyway? Have I made the worst decision of my life? Is there some dark, unknown sin of which I am unaware and for which I am being disciplined?*

All those thoughts and more crossed my mind as I met God in the wee hours of the morning to gain perspective, hear his voice, and garner enough grace to make it through another day. It was the hardest year of my life. I cried out to God, and I also just plain cried. I felt as desperate and dependent as any time in my Christian life. Two things sustained me: that promise from God, and the knowledge of his wisdom.

I had longed to grow deeper in prayer, and the multiple crises drove me to my knees. Following a founder often means disaster for the next leader, but the economic downturn created a leadership team and staff that learned to fast, cut back, and sacrifice in a way that built unity. The daughter I was so concerned about didn't just make the transition, she flourished in it. The challenges developed her faith, her gifts, and her leadership potential in ways that still amaze me.

The grown son we left behind met his future wife, married, and spent a year on staff with Campus Crusade before returning to his role as a physical therapist. My wife had a season to mourn, time to be restored, and the gift of a new church family that rallied around her in the midst of her pain. The economic downturn forced the ministry to completely change the paradigm and as a result grew from reaching 20,000 pastors and teachers in 19 countries, to reaching 90,000 pastors and teachers in over 100 countries.

We unfortunately tend to think that God's will and "ease and blessing" go hand in hand. It certainly did not for Jesus, the disciples, or the church throughout history. But somehow, the difficulty and pain we experienced caused us to question God's will and wisdom. I'm reminded of Jesus words, "Unless a kernel of wheat falls to the ground and dies, it remains only a single seed. But if it dies, it produces many seeds" (John 12:24).

Life isn't always easy, but God in his wisdom always brings about the best possible results, by the best possible means, for the most possible people, for the longest possible time. That truth and promise from God kept me from giving up or giving in when my life seemed utterly impossible.

Live It Out—B.I.O.

"Bio" is a word that is synonymous with "life." Found in those three simple letters, B.I.O. is the key to helping you become the person God wants you to be.

B *Come BEFORE God daily.* Meet with him personally through his Word and prayer to enjoy his presence, receive his direction, and follow his will.

I *Do Life IN COMMUNITY weekly.* Structure your week to personally connect in safe relationships that provide love, support, transparency, challenge, and accountability.

O *ON MISSION 24/7.* Cultivate a mindset to "live out" Jesus's love for others through acts of sacrifice and service at home, work, play, and church.

Come BEFORE God

- Write the following definition on a notecard, smartphone, or tablet and place it where you will read it when you get up in the morning and when you go to bed. Don't try to memorize it. Simply read it in a spirit of prayer and let the reality of God's wisdom gently pour over your soul.

> The wisdom of God tells us that God will bring about the best possible results, by the best possible means, for the most possible people, for the longest possible time.
>
> Dr. Charles Ryrie[5]

- Near the definition, write Romans 11:33–36 and meditate on that thought. Each time you read it, begin by asking, "What would it be like if I really believed that God is all-wise and has actually allowed my circumstances for his good purposes? What if *everything* in my life is part of his wise plan?"

> Oh, the depth of the riches both of the wisdom and knowledge of God! How unsearchable are His judgments and unfathomable His ways! For WHO HAS KNOWN THE MIND OF THE LORD, OR WHO BECAME HIS COUNSELOR? Or WHO HAS FIRST GIVEN TO HIM THAT IT MIGHT BE PAID BACK TO HIM AGAIN? For from Him and through Him and to Him are all things. To Him be the glory forever. Amen. (Rom. 11:33–36 NASB)

- Join me in making the following prayer your own for the next seven days:

O Lord God, infinite in wisdom and knowledge, as I consider your purposes and your plans, grant that I might

- *live in total awe and reverence for you,*

- *feast daily upon your Word,*

- *ask for your wisdom in every situation, and*

- *trust you completely when life doesn't make sense.*

Let me know your will and help me to follow it wholeheartedly, remembering that you already know every ripple of every action throughout history, now and forever. Because of your wisdom, you freely offer your best in every situation, and you provide it to all who ask. So today, I ask. In Jesus's name, Amen.

Do Life IN Community

- Wise living involves asking God for wisdom specially. How can you specially pray for a friend or loved one? Pray with them for God's wisdom in their life.

Be ON Mission

- Spending regular time in God's Word is essential to wise living. What practical steps are you making to gain God's wisdom through Scripture? Consider going on a media fast.

8

THE JUSTICE OF GOD

Far be it from you to do such a thing—to kill the righteous
with the wicked, treating the righteous and the wicked alike.
Far be it from you! Will not the Judge of all the earth do right?

Genesis 18:25

On a beautiful September morning, Jim boarded his usual commuter train for the city. When he left home, the kids were stirring, still getting used to the regimen of school mornings after a relaxing summer schedule. He had a special gesture for each of them: a shoulder squeeze for his teenage daughter, a ruffling of hair for the young boy who was rapidly catching up in height, and a tight hug from his little princess who still thought Daddy could leap over tall buildings in a single bound—even the very tall building he worked in. He kissed his wife and offered a muffled "I love you" around the toasted bagel he ate on his way to the station.

The subway was packed. He chuckled again over the good fortune of having his exit station right under the building that housed his offices.

He walked through the station, up the stairs, and into the lobby of the World Trade Center, where a bank of elevators waited to take him and thousands of others to high floors. Jim arrived at his office and placed his coffee cup on the desk. He took off his coat and, as was his habit, paused before he sat down to glance out the window over New York City back toward home. A blur distracted him and he turned just in time to notice that an airplane was about to collide with the building. That was his last conscious thought.

We've all heard the stories. To avoid intruding on a specific family's personal tragedy, I've combined in Jim's story some common elements of real-life victims. Nearly three thousand innocent people going through their normal routines were killed that day in the attack. Thousands more survived. People of all kinds died, and people of all kinds lived. Who let those misguided fools commandeer two jetliners and fly them into the World Trade Center? Who decided on the list of victims and the list of survivors? Those of us who watched the horrific scenes felt the questions bubble up along with our fear, anger, and confusion. Where was God in the middle of that carnage? Why would he allow such a bad thing to happen to so many good people?

Those same feelings and questions resurface in the wake of the shootings in San Bernardino, California. Fourteen innocent people enjoying an office Christmas party were violently killed by extremists who acted on behalf of their god. Where was God? Why did he allow this violent tragedy to happen?

Smaller tragedies provoke the same big question. I was walking up the aisle one night before a church service in which I was going to speak on this subject when a man got my attention. I leaned over to greet him and he pointed at the bulletin and said, "I'm glad you're going to talk about this."

"Why?" I asked.

"I lost my wife about two and a half years ago." He sighed. "She was the picture of health. We were enjoying the greatest years of our marriage. Then she got cancer and boom, she was gone. I still struggle with why." The question had been nagging him. How could something so devastating be allowed to happen?

It seems like that question comes up in conversation almost daily. So does its twin—why do good things happen to bad people? Sometimes that one bothers me even more than the first.

Even folks who have no interest in God shake their heads in amazement. We all come to the same conclusion when we think about these events: Life is not fair! Our gut feeling tells us it *ought* to be fair, and we're deeply disappointed when it isn't. Especially when we're on the receiving end of the unfairness.

Those who don't believe in God are stuck with their feelings. They don't have anywhere to go with them, other than trying to work things out right now—which is often futile. They may want to hold someone ultimately responsible for injustices, but they have already decided there is no one. You can't hold someone who doesn't exist responsible for an unfair world.

Those of us who do believe in God often face two difficulties. We have to explain our own feelings of anger and disappointment, and we have to answer the questions others ask us:

- How can you believe in God, especially a good and just God, when there is so much lack of justice in the world?

- If life isn't fair, and God created life, then how do we know *he* is fair?

- How do you know God is just and that you're not going to get a raw deal from him?

- How can you believe in the wisdom of God when he allows bad things to happen to good people and good things to happen to bad people?

- How can you trust God when the world he controls is so obviously unfair?

These questions resonate within us. Even when we have experienced years of God's faithfulness and think our relationship with him is secure, one raw deal can make us ask those questions again. In order to answer them, we have to reach an understanding of some basics, and the attribute of God's justice is one of them.

Defining the Justice of God

Dictionaries use the following words to define justice: righteousness, lawfulness, honesty, integrity, fairness, and impartiality. Justice involves an uncompromising and unwavering allegiance to a standard. Our understanding of justice tends to emphasize this idea of an external set of rules or laws that must be followed. When it comes to God's justice, however, this understanding doesn't work. Justice is not a standard God follows; he *is* the standard. He is not accountable to justice because justice flows from him. It's part of who he is.

Notice what A. W. Tozer says about the justice of God:

Quick Definition Justice embodies the idea of moral equity, and iniquity is the exact opposite; it is *in*-equity, the absence of equality from human thoughts and acts. Judgment is the application of equity to moral situations, and may be favorable or unfavorable according to whether the one under examination has been equitable or inequitable in heart and conduct.[1]

In other words, justice means that people are going to get what they deserve based on God's clear and full understanding of what they did and why they did it. We may be accustomed to legal tricks, technicalities, and excuses in human courtrooms, but there will be none of that before God. He knows every intimate detail of the case.

In order to recognize God's justice, we need to develop both a biblical worldview and a detailed understanding of biblical revelation. The priceless results from a study of justice will include a deeper grasp of what it means to worship a just God in a fallen world.

History and the Justice of God

Let's review the biblical worldview. Imagine an infinite line that represents eternity past and future—it's a line with no ends. Human history as we know it would be represented by a tiny one-inch segment on this line. Somewhere within an infinite eternity God chose to create the earth and humankind in space-time history on the one-inch segment.

The first two chapters in Genesis tell about the beginning of time and the universe. In those early days of the creation, the righteous God judges justly over a perfect environment. The first humans have regular, direct access to God. The world is a paradise.

But in Genesis 3, Adam and Eve attempted a coup under the influence of a fallen and disgraced angel named Lucifer. Instead of lashing out against God with violence, they merely disobeyed his direct command. They challenged his authority over his creation. They ate forbidden fruit and caused the fall of Creation. Sin entered the world, and into every human who came after, and the whole history of humanity from that point in time forward became twisted and distorted. That was the first judgment, when God judged us for our rebellion. God's special relationship with fallen humanity does not close again until we get to Revelation 20—the last judgment. Genesis 3 and Revelation 20 serve as the bookends of a long story about a just and loving God working out redemption for a fallen world. Outside of those bookends, perfection, holiness, and justice reign. Between them, a lot of things are unresolved—and unfair. When the book closes on sinful history, a new everlasting history will continue in a new heaven and new earth.

We are living in that brief segment of time during which a holy, just, good, compassionate, and sovereign God is interacting with a fallen world. Our world is already under judgment. Not a single moment of life is untouched by sin. Though God longs for us to see him accurately, our perspective between the first sin and the final judgment is distorted. Until we step out of this life into eternity, we will experience the effects of sin: decay and death on every side. That's why it is so important that we understand how a perfect, just God operates within a system that has been corrupted by rebellion. For that we return to the Scriptures and pick up the story within the parentheses.

God's Justice in History

God's justice is clearly revealed in the Bible's early chapters—God judges Cain for Abel's murder, he judges the world for the epidemic of sin that led to the flood, and he judges the arrogance of Babel. But we get a unique view of his justice in Genesis 18:25, our theme verse for this chapter.

You probably know the story. God saw the wickedness of Sodom and Gomorrah and determined to judge them for it. We get a glimpse into the mind of God when he says, "Shall I hide from Abraham what I am about to do?" (Gen. 18:17). He decided to let Abraham know about his plan to destroy the two cities. But there was a complication that affected Abraham. He felt that the well-deserved judgment of Sodom and Gomorrah would put Abraham's nephew Lot and his family in undeserved danger.

As we pick up the conversation in 18:25, God has told Abraham of the impending judgment. Abraham responds: "Far be it from you that you should do such a thing. To kill the righteous with the wicked? Treating the righteous and the wicked alike? Far be it from you! Will not the judge of the earth do right?"

Remember that this is centuries before the Ten Commandments. The father of our faith, living in a polytheistic world and having no written revelation, instinctively knows something about the character of God.

"Will the judge of all the earth not judge righteously?" he asks. By faith, Abraham knew God's character enough to know that there was a standard for how to treat both evil and good. And on the basis of that knowledge, he interceded in a way that allowed Lot and his family to be saved. God was willing to withhold judgment as long as there was an influencing core of righteous people. In this particular case, Abraham's negotiations revealed that if ten righteous men could still be found in the cities, they would be spared. He understood what it meant to worship a just God in an unjust world.

The Scriptures consistently remind us that justice is among the attributes we can trust God to exhibit. "Clouds and thick darkness surround him; righteousness and justice are the foundation of his throne" (Ps. 97:2). There are dozens of verses about God's justice in the Old and New Testament, but I like this one because "clouds and thick darkness," convey the idea of mystery. We can't understand everything about God, but here's what we can count on. His righteousness (truth and goodness) and his justice (fairness) are the foundations of his throne. And what does a king do from his throne? He pronounces his royal decrees and he executes judgment. God cannot be understood apart from his justice.

Life during the brief segment of human history may not always be fair. But when life inside and outside the segment are taken into account together, God's justice will be perfect. In the big picture, he makes all things right. We can trust the decisions about immediate or delayed judgment to God's wisdom.

J. I. Packer helps us face the fact that a central part of justice is the idea of retribution. God has structured reality in such a way that we understand that actions lead to consequences. Good actions bring good results; bad actions bring bad results. This truth in the basic pattern of life points us toward the Creator's character. Packer notes:

> It becomes clear that the Bible's proclamation of God's work as Judge is part of its witness to his character. . . . It shows us also that the heart of the justice which expresses God's nature is *retribution*, the rendering to persons what they have deserved; for this is the essence of a judge's task. To reward good with good, and evil with evil, is natural to God.

So when the New Testament speaks of the final judgment, it always represents it in terms of retribution. God will judge all people, it says, according to their works.[2]

The heart of the concept of judgment is this: everyone will get what he or she deserves. God is a righteous judge, and though the world is not fair, God is. Between this life and the life to come, you and I can know that no person who has ever lived will get a raw deal—even if it looks that way right now. God has proven and will prove that he is a righteous Judge.

How Does God Reveal His Justice to Us?

Inside the parameters of world history, we find—with the guidance of Scripture—several distinct ways in which God reminds us of his just nature. In fact, we ought to be humbled by the way God continually delays justice in order to give people abundant opportunities to turn to him. Peter tells us, "But do not forget this one thing, dear friends: With the Lord a day is like a thousand years, and a thousand years are like a day. The Lord is not slow in keeping his promise, as some understand slowness. He is patient with you, not wanting anyone to perish, but everyone to come to repentance" (2 Pet. 3:8–9). Any plan we have to stand before God and tell him we didn't have enough chances to acknowledge him will be exposed in the harsh light of the truth.

Through the Natural Order

God has left plenty of clues about justice in the natural order. In Romans 1:18, Paul lays out the case for the gospel as the only hope for a world awaiting sentencing by the just Judge. "The wrath of God is being revealed from heaven against all the godlessness and wickedness of men who suppress the truth by their wickedness." When the Bible speaks of God's wrath, it is referring to his righteous, passionate anger against evil. In this case, the standard of truth was deliberately ignored by the human race, so God turned his anger against the wrongdoers. The next verses provide the evidence behind God's judgment: "What may be known about God is plain to them, because God has made it plain to them. For since the creation of the world God's invisible qualities—his eternal power and divine nature—have been clearly seen, being understood from what has been made, so that men are without excuse" (Rom. 1:19–20). Ignorance is not an excuse for shunning God's character.

I played a lot of basketball when I was growing up. There are a few dirty moves a player can use to compensate for a disadvantage in size. Being very small and skinny, I quickly learned them. When a defender would reach for the ball, I would spin toward him and stick out my elbow so it would catch him right in the nose. I remember a very large guard whose nose began to bleed after my elbow hit it. Before he left the court, he warned me very clearly: "Just remember, everything that goes around, comes around." The ref may not have seen my move, but the player was claiming a higher law.

That instinct is universal. In eastern religions, they call it karma—and since it clearly doesn't play out in this life, there must be many lives to settle the score. In western religions, it's a matter for the afterlife. In any case, it's ingrained in us: there is a higher law of justice.

This basic understanding of cause and effect is written into our psyche from the time we were created. We are most prone to claim that law when we are on the receiving end of one of life's unfair moments. Even a casual observer, regardless of culture or background, notices that same basic philosophy anywhere in the world: when you do good things to people, good things come your way; and when you do bad things to people, bad things come your way. Although we can all cite exceptions to this principle of life under the sun, none of us can deny that it is the normal pattern—nor can we deny the personal outrage we experience when this life principle appears not to be operating consistently.

Through the Human Heart

God has also revealed justice in the way he has made the human heart. One of the premises of Romans is that an intuitive awareness of God is built into the order of creation. Paul builds a strong case that all people, regardless of their religion or morality, know they have fallen short of God's glory. Romans 2:14–16 focuses on people who have nothing but an internal sense of right and wrong:

> (Indeed, when Gentiles, who do not have the law, do by nature things required by the law, they are a law for themselves, even though they do not have the law, since they show that the requirements of the law are written on their hearts, their consciences also bearing witness, and their thoughts now accusing, now even defending them.) This will take place on the day when God will judge men's secrets through Jesus Christ, as my gospel declares.

All people in all places—even those who have never heard a "thou shall not" from God—have an internal law that tells them right from wrong. When they violate that law, their conscience lets them know. They feel guilty.

There's a good example of this principle in Acts 28:3–6, which records an event that occurred during Paul's last trip to Rome. He was shipwrecked on an island filled with pagans. The frozen and soaked survivors built a fire. Luke describes what happened next:

> Paul gathered a pile of brushwood and, as he put it on the fire, a viper, driven out by the heat, fastened itself on his hand. When the islanders saw the snake hanging from his hand, they said to each other, "This man must be a murderer; for though he escaped from the sea, Justice has not allowed him to live." But Paul shook the snake off into the fire and suffered no ill effects. The people expected him to swell up or suddenly fall dead, but after waiting a long time and seeing nothing unusual happen to him, they changed their minds and said he was a god.

Seeing Paul's misfortune, the local people immediately reached a natural conclusion. If justice went to such great lengths to get him, he must have been a very bad man indeed. Then when they saw that no harm came to him, they reached for the second conclusion available in their worldview—Paul must be a god! Even to unenlightened minds, the only alternative to the law of cause and effect involves the supernatural.

C. S. Lewis was probably the greatest Christian apologist of the last century. He frequently confessed that the unavoidable sense of oughtness was a chink in his atheistic armor. It bothered him that he couldn't explain humanity's moral senses naturally. God used that chink in the armor to bring him to faith. In his book *Mere Christianity* he writes,

> These, then are the two points I want to make. First, that human beings, all over the earth, have this curious idea that they ought to behave in a certain way, and they cannot get rid of it. Secondly, that they do not in fact behave that way. They know the Law of Nature, yet they break it. These two facts are the foundation for all clear thinking about ourselves and the universe we live in.[3]

The human heart personalizes what we see in the created order. Not only is there a law of cause and effect, a force for justice loose in the universe. There are also personal aspects to that justice. People who violate the rules will experience negative consequences, and those who play by the rules will be rewarded. We can probably think of many instances when we've heard someone say, "Well, I must be living right!" or "It serves her right!" This personal side of the law of cause and effect brings into the picture the possibility of someone personal backing up the law. And that brings us to God's role as the source of justice.

Through His Role as Judge

We have a statue of a woman wearing a blindfold to illustrate the impartiality of justice. But when we think of a judge, we want someone who sees, hears, and thinks very clearly. It comes as no surprise that the Creator of everything—including that sense of justice in us—also claims to be the judge of all the earth. Scripture reveals not only his ongoing role as Judge in the midst of history, but confidently declares that God will eventually pass final judgment on all people in all of history.

The Bible allows no ambiguity about God's position as Judge. According to Hebrews 12:23, "You have come to God, the judge of all men." Recognizing God as Judge should be sobering to us, but if we know that he is also on our side and has intervened for us, we can face judgment with confidence. Paul expressed that sense of comfort and longing when he wrote to Timothy. Although Paul was ready to die, his last letter to his son in the faith included these upbeat words: "Now there is in store for me the crown of righteousness, which the Lord, the righteous Judge, will award to me on that day—and not only to me, but also to all who have longed for his appearing" (2 Tim. 4:8). We can know that

God has made a way to satisfy his just character as well as his loving, gracious, overwhelming goodness. We see this most powerfully when we see the cross of Christ.

Through the Cross

Scripture explains that the central reason for the cross was for God to show the whole world his justice. "God presented him [Jesus] as a sacrifice of atonement through faith in his blood. He did this to demonstrate *his justice*, because in his forbearance he had left the sins committed beforehand unpunished" (Rom. 3:25, emphasis added). God presented his own Son as a sacrifice. The word *atonement* literally means a covering. Christ's life, offered on the cross, accomplished something for us that could not be accomplished any other way. It "covered" our sin, not in the sense of hiding it or pretending it didn't happen, but in the sense that our extreme offense against a holy God was replaced by that sacrificial offering. Instead of requiring us to experience his retribution for sin, God sent Jesus as our substitute. Our "faith in his blood" allows us to get under Christ's atoning covering. We believe Jesus suffered, bled, and died in our place.

Paul anticipates a question about "what happens to those who lived before Christ" by describing God's "forbearance" regarding past sins. The cross of Christ stands as the centerpiece of history; its shadow of forgiveness covers both the past and the future. Christ's death atoned for those who trusted in God's plan and mercy beforehand, even as it provides atonement for those of us who live centuries later.

Paul completes the thought in verse 26: "He did it to demonstrate his justice at the present time, so as to be just and the one who justifies those who have faith in Jesus." God didn't experience an internal conflict of feelings over us, his justice demanding our punishment while his goodness longed to rescue us. He didn't choose one attribute over another. He satisfied all of them in the same moment by placing himself on the cross. Through the cross, God's qualities converged. He is shown to be supremely just in passing sentence over all human sin, and supremely merciful in being the justifier who covers those who trust him.

Perhaps you've thought you can never really understand what happened at the cross. It's true that there will always be a mystery surrounding that central moment in history, but you can still grasp enough of the significance to change your life forever. Think about what occurred when Jesus was hanging there and cried out, "My God, my God, why have you forsaken me?"

God the Father, who is holy and pure, who has an infinite relationship with God the Son and God the Holy Spirit, at that moment placed all the sin of all humankind on Christ and turned away. Then the Father's just wrath was poured out on the Son. Jesus, who lived a perfect life, bore your sin and mine precisely when God executed judgment on it.

Allow me to give you a present-day picture that will help you grasp what the Scripture teaches. Suppose I had been convicted of a crime and sentenced to the electric chair. Imagine that just before the executioner pushed the button, Jesus said, "Stop! Ingram deserves to die, but I'll take his place." They would unstrap me and let Jesus take the seat. The executioner would turn on the juice, and Jesus would die. The judge would say, "Ingram goes free; his penalty has been paid." Because God is a righteous Judge, that's what Jesus did for us. He suffered judgment for sin and set us free from its awful consequences.

The awesome, uncompromising, unrelenting justice of God is completely satisfied by the cross. When we think we can "get right with God" in any other way, we fool ourselves and dangerously underestimate the grotesque nature of rebellion. The Christian life is not about going to church, learning to pray, reading the Bible, having a nice family, giving a little money, giving a little time, supporting the United Way, and making the world a better place. That's a religion called moralism! There's nothing wrong with these things in themselves. But if we believe they make us right with God, we've missed the whole point of our faith.

What God's justice demanded, his love provided. And he provided it for you and for me at the cross. Jesus died in your place as your substitute. You can accept the free gift of his work on the cross by faith, have your well-deserved penalty be paid by Jesus, and trust that all his righteousness will come from him to you. Or there's an alternative: you can say, "I'm going to live my way, and I don't want God to have any say in it."

This insistence on our own way can take the form of passive or active rebellion. Procrastination is a passive rebellion. Many people say to themselves, "Someday, some way, I'll get around to Christ. I know God really exists but I'm doing my own thing for now." This lack of response, this passive rebellion, is in essence rejecting Christ and his offer of forgiveness and a new life. Active rebellion is more blatant. It's an adamant stance toward God. "I don't believe in God and I don't care about God. I deny creation, I deny the witness in my heart, I trust only in me!" In the eyes of God's justice, both subtle and blatant forms of rebellion fall under judgment.

Seeing God as he longs for us to see him will always involve the cross. Unless we take shelter under the sacrifice of Jesus, we are exposed to God's justice. Any other response than faith in Christ's atonement receives God's full judgment. Rebellion in any form eventually leaves a person with the devastating effects of God's justice in the tragic form of eternal retribution.

Through the Promise of Eternal Retribution

The final and most sobering way God's justice is revealed is in the promise of eternal retribution. We already saw in an earlier quote from J. I. Packer that a significant part of our understanding of justice involves the principle of retribution. Retribution simply means you get something for what you do—the account is settled. It often carries a negative overtone and can be used as a synonym for vengeance. If our debts and offenses involve an eternal being, then retribution takes on eternal consequences. The Bible teaches that retribution applies both to believers and to unbelievers.

The retribution promised to believers has an important limit. Once we come to know Christ and have accepted the free gift of his atonement, the Spirit dwells within us, we're a brand-new creation, and our salvation is sealed. But the moment you begin to live your new life, God says,

> I have an agenda for you. I'm giving you X amount of time, energy, money, spiritual gifts, background, position, and personality. And since you came to Jesus, you're going to meet him as Judge when you get to the end of your life. I'm not going to judge you for your sin, because that was judged at the cross. You're a believer, and you're heaven bound. But I *am* going to do an evaluation of your life. I will ask, "Child, what did you do with everything I gave you?"

The One who knows every secret of our heart will evaluate us clearly and completely. Retribution will follow. We will either hear, "Well done, good and faithful servant," or we will watch as our lifelong efforts get burned up. That's a disturbing scene for Christians to think about, but it is solidly biblical. Paul describes it in 1 Corinthians 3:10–15:

By the grace God has given me, I laid a foundation as an expert builder, and someone else is building on it. But each one should be careful how he builds. For no one can lay any foundation other than the one already laid, which is Jesus Christ. If any man builds on this foundation using gold, silver, costly stones, wood, hay or straw, his work will be shown for what it is, because the Day will bring it to light. It will be revealed with fire, and the fire will test the quality of each man's work. If what he has built survives, he will receive his reward. If it is burned up, he will suffer loss; he himself will be saved, but only as one escaping through the flames.

If you really want to absorb the implications, read this passage carefully at least twice. The apostle was clearly speaking to believers. The "Day" to which he refers is judgment day. When gold, silver, and precious stones are exposed to fire, they're purified. When wood, hay, and stubble are exposed to fire, they vanish. There will be fire on judgment day, and it will test *everything*. Every believer will stand before the judgment seat of Christ, and we will either be purified and rewarded or we will see the smoldering ruins of misused gifts. I'll leave the details for the theologians to argue about, but this is what's clear from Scripture—the fact of heaven for us will not change, but the quality of our heavenly experience will. It will be directly proportional to our stewardship in this life. In eternity, the principle of retribution will affect us one way or another.

As we mentioned above, retribution also applies to unbelievers. "It is appointed for men to die once and after this comes judgment" (Heb. 9:27 NASB). Death and hell may be unpleasant subjects, but that shouldn't stop us from talking about them. They are unavoidable. In fact, death and hell are not even negative subjects when properly understood. Hell is the clearest evidence that God is serious about preserving the dignity and freedom of humanity. Because he respects our will, he has reserved a place for all those who say, "I am the captain of my own ship, I will live my own life, and no one can tell me what to do." We can't love someone unless we can choose to accept him or reject him. God treats us as free moral agents and will honor our rejection of him for all eternity. C. S. Lewis was right when he described only two basic views of life—those who say to God, "My will be done!" and those who say to God, "Thy will be done."[4] One of those statements represents your life. Hell preserves the dignity and the freedom of people who stiff-arm God. God's justice says, "I'll create a place of retribution so anyone who wishes to stay away from me can do so." Hell is serious, and it's as real as heaven.

Those who end up in hell know the answer to the question that's often asked: "How could a good God send anyone to hell?" A good God *doesn't* send anybody to hell. A good God sent his Son so that no one would have to go to hell. Anyone who goes to hell has said, "God, I don't want your will or your Son. I want my will." God honors that heartfelt desire. Those in hell have chosen to be there.

God has revealed and continues to reveal his justice in many ways. The clues are compelling, but they still require a response. We have looked at the big picture, but we now need to look at the immediate, practical response of your heart as you consider God's justice. As you read the descriptions of the causes for negative retribution both for believers and unbelievers, you may have felt a shaft of truth pierce your soul. That insight requires a personal response from you.

How Are We to Respond to God's Justice?

If you want to remain in a place of unbelief or do-it-my-way Christianity, that in itself is a response. I would simply remind you that if you stay in that frame of mind, there will be eternal consequences—negative retribution. If, however, you are longing to see God as he is longing to be seen by you, responding to his justice will certainly be a significant part of that change in your life. Here is how to do life God's way:

Choose to embrace Jesus.

As with every significant step of growth in the Christian life, we begin at the cross. It doesn't matter whether you're coming there for the first time or returning with a deeper understanding. Responding to God's justice involves embracing Jesus as our Savior now rather than fearing him as our righteous Judge later. You are choosing to do what all people on the planet will eventually be compelled to do, even against their will. The Scripture tells us that you and I and everyone else will someday bow and acknowledge that Jesus is Lord (Phil. 2:9–11). For some it will be the most tremendous, awesome, and encouraging moment of their existence. They will finally get to see face-to-face the One they have trusted for years. For others it will be a terrible moment of bitter truth when they wonder, "Why didn't I respond?"

Historically, that moment of truth may come years from now, but for any one of us, it could come in the next moment. The instant you die, you will fast-forward to that point of judgment. If you are living in obedient fellowship with Jesus as Savior, you've got nothing to worry about. If you are living apart from Christ or ignoring his presence in your life, an unpleasant retribution is waiting.

The invitation to choose to embrace Jesus is not about being better or being religious. Don't be fooled by that dangerous detour. It's considering life to the point where you can honestly say to God, "I understand that Jesus died to pay for my sin and to satisfy your justice, and today

I turn from my sin. I repent, I ask you to come into my life and forgive me based on Jesus's work, and I now want to follow you with all of my heart all the days of my life."

Jesus himself offered a powerful confirmation of what just occurred if you prayed a prayer like that.

> Moreover, the Father judges no one, but has entrusted all judgment to the Son, that all may honor the Son just as they honor the Father. He who does not honor the Son does not honor the Father, who sent him.
>
> I tell you the truth, whoever hears my word and believes him who sent me has eternal life and will not be condemned; he has crossed over from death to life. (John 5:22–24)

Let those phrases ring in your soul— "*has* eternal life" and "*has* crossed over from death to life." When someone asks, "What's going to happen when you die?" you can answer, "I'm going to start fully enjoying the eternal life I already have!"

Refuse to seek vengeance.

Beyond the cross, God's justice takes on very practical implications for daily living in an unfair world. A second response to knowing that he alone is Judge is a decisive refusal to seek revenge.

There are Christians living with bitterness and unresolved anger toward former bosses, former friends, rebellious children, bad parents, and people who have abused them. As real as those feelings are, those responses are created when we take God's place as judge over the injustices in life. It's a wasted effort, and it's sinful. God's Word is clear:

Do not repay anyone evil for evil. Be careful to do what is right in the eyes of everybody. If it is possible, as far as it depends on you, live at peace with everyone. Do not take revenge, my friends, but leave room for God's wrath, for it is written: "It is mine to avenge; I will repay," says the Lord. On the contrary:

> "If your enemy is hungry, feed him;
>   if he is thirsty, give him something to drink.
> In doing this, you will heap burning coals on his head."
> Do not be overcome by evil, but overcome evil with good. (Rom.
>   12:17–21)

These may be some of the most neglected instructions among Christians. Holding on to offenses and seeking vengeance keeps thousands trapped in a cycle of bondage. Thirst for vengeance puts us in the dangerous place of playing God. It's a form of idolatry. Why? Because it rejects God's clear offer to take care of everything in due time. He has promised to balance the scales. If people need to go to the spiritual woodshed, he'll take them there. Instead of seeking vengeance, we are to say, "Lord, you take care of that."

If you're like most of us, seeking vengeance won't be your biggest issue. *Thinking* vengeance will be. When someone hands you a raw deal, your anger and bitterness may not drive you to revenge, but they can still prompt some pretty unwholesome thoughts. Many people envision bad things happening to someone who deserves them, or secretly celebrate when someone who once inflicted pain is now in pain himself. If you've ended up on the unfair end of a divorce, a broken contract, an abusive relationship, an insult, or a job cut, you've probably wrestled with vengeance in your mind, even if you've never considered acting it out. That's a more subtle form of being "overcome by evil," and God's Word addresses it just as clearly.

When we harbor bitterness, we are harming ourselves, not the person we resent. God wants us to be at peace within as well as without. Whatever the issue is, let it go. You don't have to settle the score in your own mind. Consciously and deliberately remind yourself that in his timing, God is able to take care of the situation fairly and fully. You can always trust him to do that.

Obviously, there are situations along the way that may require some kind of response from us. This is where a wise believer will use Scripture and godly counsel to take action that God would want. But there's a difference between addressing a situation and taking revenge. Vengeance is God's job—refuse to do it yourself, either psychologically or physically. Trusting a just God with that is a powerful way to worship him in a fallen world. (For video resources on forgiveness, visit truespirituality online.org.)

Take comfort in God's justice.

The third response goes hand in hand with the second. Instead of taking vengeance, Christians can take comfort when they encounter injustice, knowing God will eventually balance the scales. That knowledge is comforting when:

- people gossip behind your back

- someone hits your car and doesn't have insurance

- you get ripped off financially

- you get passed over for a promotion

- your spouse walks out on you, and you find out he or she was shacking up with someone else

- a drunk driver hits someone you love and changes your life forever

- you get a raw deal

- you're blatantly cheated

- a best friend betrays a confidence

Always take comfort in God's justice when facing an unfair hardship.

For practical encouragement, go to Psalm 73. Asaph says he almost fell when he saw "the prosperity of the wicked." Good things happened to bad people, and it really got under his skin. Then in verse 17, he entered God's sanctuary and saw things from a better perspective. He quit looking only at life between the parentheses and got a glimpse of the whole picture. By the end of the psalm, he is content with God as his "portion." God is his strength and his refuge, and he knows things will end according to God's perfect justice.

Like Asaph, you can say, "Comfort me, God. I rest in your justice." If there's any person on the face of the earth that went through injustice, it was Jesus. He understands, so talk to him about it. He'll cry with you about it, console you in it, and love you through it.

Meditate on the effects of God's final judgment.

The final response to God's justice is to meditate deeply on the reality of the judgment seat of Christ—the promise of spiritual reward and loss. "For we must all appear before the judgment seat of Christ, that each one may receive what is due him for the things done while in the body, whether good or bad" (2 Cor. 5:10).

If you are a believer in Christ, I want you to do a heart check. Ask yourself this question: If I continue to live for ten, thirty, or fifty years with the same priorities, the same use of my money, the same use of my time, the same use of my gifts, the same passions, and my energy going where it has been going, will I hear a "well done" when I come and bow before Christ? Or will I hear, "What in the world did you do with what I gave you? How, in light of all eternity and what I did on the cross, could you live such a self-centered, self-focused, pleasure-seeking life and actually be one of my children? You are saved and forgiven and you will spend eternity with me, but you were an embarrassment to the kingdom of God."

In other words, will Jesus point to your life as a beautiful building that honors him? Or will he point to a house going up in flames because it wasn't built of anything eternal?

If you think that living the same way you're living today is going to produce different results, you've been misled. Now would be the time to review your priorities, your relationships, your money, your focus, and your energy. This is a good time to adjust them in such a way that when you stand before the judgment seat of Christ, he will rise and embrace you as you have embraced him. You'll hear him say, "Great to see you! Way to go. I'm proud of you!"

Does this mean you'll be perfect? Of course not. You will experience ups and downs and lots of failures. God's justice will help you see them clearly and humbly repent of them rather than excuse them. His justice will prevent you from being proud and hardhearted. It will shape you into a person who looks a lot like Jesus.

My Experience with the Justice of God

The practical impact God's justice can have on our everyday lives is amazing. While I was working on this chapter, God provided a graphic opportunity to teach me to rest in his justice as two local characters ripped me off.

During my time living in Atlanta I learned that pine straw is used for ground cover around shrubs, bushes, and open areas under trees. I had never heard of pine straw before, but soon learned—with my wife's encouragement—that we needed to cover those bare areas in our front yard. So, one Saturday morning we started the project and learned the fine art of pine straw disbursement. Unfortunately we ran out of both time and pine straw. I had to travel for the next two weeks, so we decided to put the project on hold.

When I returned, Theresa and I went on a breakfast date to get reconnected. On our way back home, two men in a badly beat-up pickup truck loaded with pine straw were parked on the side of the road. *What a perfect time to communicate to my wife that I care about her world*, I thought. So I stopped and asked about the pine straw. Although both men appeared dirty and unkempt and behaved strangely, I had them follow me around the corner to my house and bought thirty bales of pine straw from them. My heart went out to them, so I gave them each a good tip, a copy of a book I had written that I prayed God might use in their life, and I wished them well.

Hours later as we attempted to spread the pine straw, it was obvious that it was nothing like what we had purchased before. It was dried out, filled with debris, hard to spread, and grossly discolored. We had been taken. An attempt to reach out to a couple of surly figures with $100 and two books was repaid by one royal raw deal.

In years past, my response would likely have been intense anger and complaining followed by an all-out strategy to find those men and get my money back. But as I thought of the justice of God, I could rest in the facts that he knows the score and life is bigger than pine straw. I got to reach out to two men and give good for evil. I got to learn about the difference between good pine straw and bad pine straw. I was able to let it go and not obsess over the $100. Why? Because my God is good, he is sovereign, and in this case, I can trust that he is just.

I wrote those words and that story in the first edition of this book over ten years ago. It may sound trite to many of you who think losing $100 is not that big of a deal. But some of us have a very strong justice gene in our personal makeup and personality and we desperately want things to be fair and right.

Little did I know that this event was God's training wheels for the most difficult experience of injustice in my life only a few years later. The issues were not small, the amount of money was not small, and the level of trust violated was astronomical. I spent two years in agony seeking to make things right and to see justice done; all to no avail with regard to my personal satisfaction.

By God's grace and the wise counsel and support of mature brothers in Christ, I released the entire situation, forgave completely those in question, trusted God to restore whatever he chose to restore, and was rescued from my own anxiety and resentment. Why? Because life will never be fair on this fallen planet, but my God is just and I can entrust my real and perceived injustice to him.

Miraculously, God provided. Miraculously, I saw and was willing to face the hypocrisy of my demand for justice for others while pleading for mercy for my own failures. Miraculously, I have experienced genuine reconciliation with those involved and can testify that healing and hope are possible even in seemingly impossible situations.

Live It Out—B.I.O.

"Bio" is a word that is synonymous with "life." Found in those three simple letters, B.I.O. is the key to helping you become the person God wants you to be.

B *Come BEFORE God daily.* Meet with him personally through his Word and prayer to enjoy his presence, receive his direction, and follow his will.

I *Do Life IN COMMUNITY weekly.* Structure your week to personally connect in safe relationships that provide love, support, transparency, challenge, and accountability.

O *ON MISSION 24/7.* Cultivate a mindset to "live out" Jesus's love for others through acts of sacrifice and service at home, work, play, and church.

Come BEFORE God

- Write the following definition on a notecard, smartphone, or tablet and place it where you will read it when you get up in the morning and when you go to bed. Don't try to memorize it. Simply read it in a spirit of prayer and let the reality of God's justice pour over your soul.

God is just. That means all he is and all he does is accomplished with perfect integrity, fairness, righteousness, and impartiality. Justice is not a standard God follows; he is the standard. Though full of goodness, infinite in love, and merciful to the repentant, God's justice demands moral equity and eternal retribution for deeds done in the body. God's justice means no one will receive a "raw deal" in the final analysis. I can trust that he will one day balance the scales.

- Near the definition, write Romans 12:17–21 and meditate on that thought. Each time you read it, begin by asking, "What would it be like if I really believed that God is just and will make everything right in the end? How would that change my attitudes and responses to others?"

  Never pay back evil for evil to anyone. Respect what is right in the sight of all men. If possible, so far as it depends on you, be at peace with all men. Never take your own revenge, beloved, but leave room for the wrath of God, for it is written, "VENGEANCE IS MINE, I WILL REPAY," says the Lord. "BUT IF YOUR ENEMY IS HUNGRY, FEED HIM, AND IF HE IS THIRSTY, GIVE HIM A DRINK; FOR IN SO DOING YOU WILL HEAP BURNING COALS ON HIS HEAD." Do not be overcome by evil, but overcome evil with good. (Rom. 12:17–21 NASB)

- Join me in making the following prayer your own for the next seven days:

  O Lord God, holy and just, as I consider your righteous judgments, grant that I might

- *learn to treasure the sacrifice and atonement of Jesus,*

- *abandon all vengeance to you and refuse to seek it on my own terms,*

- *take comfort in you when life is unfair, and*

- *remember that I will one day stand before your judgment seat.*

Help me to rest in your righteousness and defer to your justice. Because you are Judge of all the earth, I bow patiently before your authority in faith and in gratitude. In Jesus's name, Amen.

- Which one of the four responses to God's justice resonates with you in your life right now? Why?

  - Embrace Jesus

  - Refuse to seek vengeance

  - Take comfort in God's justice

  - Meditate on the effects of God's final judgment

- If you need to forgive a person who has hurt you, choose to release them, not relive the hurts.

Do Life IN Community

- If you are working through a relational hurt or conflict, ask a friend to help you on this journey.

- What are some practical ways that you can unexpectedly bless a person who has wounded you? (Rom. 12:20)

Be ON Mission

- How can forgiving those who have hurt you and taking comfort in God's justice be a means of drawing other people to Christ?

9

THE LOVE OF GOD

> How great is the love the Father has lavished on us, that we
> should be called children of God! And that is what we are!
>
> 1 John 3:1

When you teach God's Word as often as I do, you eventually get stumped when it comes to introducing a message. You want an introduction to capture the listeners' attention, introduce your main subject, and get them emotionally engaged in the journey.

I was preparing to teach on one of the greatest chapters in the Bible, and by far one of the most important messages in all of Scripture—1 Corinthians 13—but I was stuck. After multiple futile attempts, crumpled pieces of paper on the floor, and some intense prayer, I sensed God giving me an idea for an introduction. Honestly, it seemed risky, even a little wacky. It *could* be a powerful way to launch the message on love; or it could *really bomb*.

As I stepped toward the pulpit, I asked people to lean back in their chairs and relax. I walked around to the edge of the platform and said, "I'd like to try a little experiment. I'm going to sing an old song. It's an oldie and a goldie with a great message. It isn't a Christian song, but it ought to be. So join in if you know the words and want to sing along."

So with no accompaniment, I started in on my best rendition of an old Burt Bacharach song popularized by Dionne Warwick: "What the World Needs Now." Within a few bars, hundreds had joined in. I thought they were going to start swaying back and forth. The spontaneous, eager response by young and old completely caught me off guard. I actually had to interrupt them to get them to stop.

Why? What was it about that song that so deeply resonated with every person in the room? What were the dynamics behind a group of people of all ages and backgrounds moving out of their comfort zone without warning to sing about one, singular subject . . . love? Could it be that love is really what the world needs today?

Can you imagine what would happen in your home and among your friends if you started loving them more, and they started loving each other more? I don't mean perfectly. I'd settle for 50 percent more than now. Wouldn't that be awesome?

What if that happened at work—if everyone, believers and nonbelievers alike, started loving each other 50 percent more? But why stop there? What if everyone in the Middle East, in central Africa, in the Balkans, and in downtown Los Angeles or New York started loving each other more? What if United Nations meetings were characterized more by productive discussions on tough issues than by contentious and personal attacks? What if political campaigns were filled with mutual respect rather than mudslinging? What if everyone at family get-togethers—the in-laws, the squeaky wheel that every family seems to have, the estranged siblings and parents—actually enjoyed being together because they loved each other just a little bit more?

It would be a kinder, more generous, more caring and forgiving world, and I don't think anyone would disagree with that. So what's the problem? Why isn't there more love? People say "I love you" all the time. Why hasn't the world changed? There's a problem, of course. Everyone feels love, but we don't exactly understand it. We're very selective about to whom we give it, and we're very inconsistent with it over time. We try to describe it, but we have a hard time finding the right words for it. And when it comes to God's love—the infinite, enduring, unconditional love of our heavenly Father—we really can't relate. We always try to put it into our own human terms, and our terms always fall far too short.

When I began this study on the attributes of God, I thought love would probably be the easiest to write about. I was wrong. As I have thought about God's love, I have felt more and more inadequate to put it into words. In seeking what God longs for us to see about his love, we walk on holy and mysterious ground. The idea of his love seems so familiar—until we actually start thinking about it.

I'm convinced that God's love is one of the hardest attributes for us to get a handle on. I've seen glimpses of it, but like most of us, my understanding falls short. I've done my biblical homework, and I know what the passages say, but I find myself even more tongue-tied than when I try to explain to my wife what I mean when I say "I love you." I never sense that I've done a very good job explaining it. In the same way, explaining God's love always turns into describing what is far better, deeper, and wider than words can capture. I've benefited from what others have told me about God's love, and I trust these words will encourage you to experience God's love for yourself. An ocean of his love is available, and I'm convinced that the average believer, including myself, is not even close to tapping into it—at least not as much as he wants us to. If we don't try to see God's love more and more clearly, we will not be the kind of people who make a significant difference in the world.

Three facts drive me to do the best I can to communicate the love of God:

1. Everyone is looking for love.

This quest is around us every day in the music we hear and the movies we watch. The desire is woven into the fiber of our being. From the moment we came out of the womb, we have been looking for someone to feed us, hug us, care for us, affirm us, forgive us when we mess up, support us, and tell us that we matter just as we are. Regardless of what country we are born in, or what our racial, cultural, and religious background might be, there's a universal need among human beings to be loved. Almost every one of our activities can actually be explained as an effort to preserve, enhance, or pursue love in some way. Marriages crumble because of mistakes people have made looking for love in all the wrong places. The evidence around us is clear; *everyone* is looking for love.

2. Just as there is a universal quest for love, there is a universal answer to that quest.

If everyone has the same problem, there must be a universal solution. If we all need the same kind of love, then the source of that love would have to be enormous and all-encompassing. Obviously, the only one who can love us that way is God. We may try to satisfy our need for love from other creatures like ourselves, but no one can give us the love our Creator can. God loves people everywhere, and he longs to meet our hearts' deepest needs. The God who created this planet and sustains it, the God who wove our DNA together in the womb, is the same God who loves us unconditionally, totally apart from our performance.

3. There's a tragic disconnection between the universal need and the universal answer.

On one hand, there are more than seven billion people in the world who are desperate for love; and on the other hand, there's a God with limitless resources who wants to love them. But the two hands are often far apart. The average person is not experiencing God's love.

Imagine a vast crowd representing the entire population of the globe—North America, South America, Africa, Asia, Australia, Europe—gathered in one place, standing shoulder to shoulder. For the moment, all the basic needs have been supplied: air, food, and water. Now imagine that instead of the oceans and lakes being filled with water, they are brimming with liquid love. Every stream, pond, and river holds it while the countless multitude stands oblivious to it. The depths of love, plentiful and ready for the taking, are within its reach. But somehow there's no connection between the need and the supply. *That's* the world's predicament.

There are still many people who haven't experienced the love of God because they don't even know it's available. They don't know God loves them because no one has ever showed his love to them. They would embrace it if they were aware of it, but tragically, they aren't. Imagine a landlocked person who has never seen the ocean. Maybe he's heard about it, but the words he has heard haven't captured it. What would he think when he finally saw it? It would blow his mind, wouldn't it? That's the situation of billions of people in this world; they've never recognized God's love, and it would blow their minds if they did.

Many people know about God's love—they have visited that "ocean"—but they haven't yet received it. Maybe they've stood on the shore and been told, "There's God's love." They may even believe that God loves them, but it makes no more difference than the idea of any other stranger loving them. They've never jumped into the water. They've never immersed themselves in it. They've never discovered that the water of God's love is sweet and satisfies the soul like nothing else.

There's a third group who knows about God's love and has even been to the ocean. They dove in and received a generous washing and drink from God's love, but they climbed back out and continued living as if God's love didn't make a lasting difference. They seem to think that they aren't allowed to keep visiting the beach. They have such emotional baggage and memories that they find it difficult to believe God's love is unconditional, sacrificial, giving, and totally apart from their performance. They get his love mixed up with how their parents loved them or how someone else loved them, and they just can't figure out on a daily basis how to experience a supernatural kind of love.

One noted Christian author, speaking about the problem some Christians have with receiving God's love, wrote this:

> Over the years I've come to realize that the greatest trap in our life is not success, popularity, or power, but self-rejection. Success, popularity, and power can indeed present a great temptation, but their seductive quality often comes from the way they are part of the much larger temptation to self-rejection.

> When we have come to believe in the voices that call us worthless and unlovable, then success, popularity and power are easily perceived as attractive solutions. The real trap, however, is self-rejection. . . . Self-rejection is the greatest enemy of the spiritual life because it contradicts the sacred voice that calls us the "Beloved." Being the Beloved constitutes the core truth of our existence.[1]

This chapter will involve an eighteen-inch journey for most of us—from the head to the heart. It's eighteen inches that makes the difference between standing on the beach and being in the waves. You can stand still and hope the tide of God's love comes up and catches you, or you can dive in. And it's a journey you can take wherever you are right now. My prayer is that the Spirit of God would personally take you on this trip, showing you in the next few pages how much God loves you and convincing your heart that his love is so certain that you can live by it and act on it. The trip will begin in your mind, as we clarify what we mean when we speak of the love of God and as we explore how God has revealed his love in this world. Then we will challenge our hearts to begin to beat with God's heart, sensing how much he longs for us to be immersed in his love.

Defining the Love of God

Frankly, dictionaries don't help much when it comes to defining God's love. There are so many kinds of love, and so many of them are distorted by human misperceptions, that dictionary words just don't do the job very well—at least not when it comes to God's kind of love. Dictionaries get about as close to describing love accurately as I do when I'm explaining it to my wife. So I set the dictionary aside, collected some Bible passages and favorite quotes—from A. W. Tozer, J. I. Packer, and others—and eventually came up with this working definition:

> **Quick Definition**
>
> God's love is his holy disposition toward all that he has created that compels him to express unconditional affection and selective correction to provide the highest quality of existence, both now and forever, for the object of his love.

That long sentence summarizes what I have learned so far about God's love. Let me unpack it for you, highlighting certain key words.

We have already looked at the word *holy* as one of God's attributes. It means "other" and "set apart." God doesn't love you like anyone else does—like your wife, husband, mom, dad, or one of your children. He loves you better. He loves you personally, specifically, and individually. His holy disposition, attitude, and choice is to know you by name and lean toward you.

If the kind of love that we have would barely fill a tiny vial, his would fill the oceans on a million planets. It's completely different, both in quantity and quality. God's holy disposition is directed toward all that he has created, not just the good or the obedient.

The source of this loving disposition is in God, not in the object. We don't provoke, trick, convince, earn, or win God's love. He doesn't love us because of who we are but because of who he is. His nature and character compel him to express unconditional affection toward us.

God is affectionate and gracious when we are good, and he is affectionate and gracious when we are evil. His love is tough and complete, which means it includes selective correction. God cares so much that when we move in directions that would be harmful for us, he disciplines us and brings us back in line because he wants the very best for us. He is well disposed toward us. He wants the highest quality existence we can have.

Do you realize what that means for you personally? Whatever it means to be filled to the brim with goodness and life, *that's* what God wants for you. He wants that for you now, in this life, and he wants that for you forever. When pleasures will move us toward that kind of life, that's what he gives. When pain will move us toward it, that's what he gives.

God stands ready with whatever it takes to provide his children with abundant life.

In the Bible, we find a particular word used to name the love that God exhibits: *agape*. English uses one word (*love*) in dozens of settings, but Greek has several words that often end up being translated into our language as *love*. God's *agape*-love is characterized by being giving, sacrificial, unconditional, and boundless.

Even those of us who didn't grow up with a lot of Scripture usually recognize the classic verse about God's love found in John 3:16—even if only on banners at football games: "For God so loved the world that he gave his one and only Son, that whoever believes in him shall not perish but have eternal life." Each of the characteristics listed above is illustrated by this verse. God gave sacrificially ("his one and only Son") so that anyone who believes ("whoever") could have boundless abundance ("eternal life").

One of my favorite passages helps us think about the dimensions of God's love. In Ephesians 3:17–19 Paul says, "And I pray that you, being rooted and established in love, may have power, together with all the saints, to grasp how wide and long and high and deep is the love of Christ, and to know this love that surpasses knowledge—that you may be filled to the measure of all the fullness of God." There is no instrument that can measure how much God, out of his infinite being, cares for you and wants your best.

That's hard for us to get our arms around, isn't it? We struggle to comprehend God's love. Because of our human relationships, we have been conditioned to measure love by what we do and how well we do it. Our loves are always characterized by "ifs," "maybes," and "becauses." I'll love you *if* you do this, or I love you *because* you did that. We can hardly imagine a love without conditions.

Theologian Charles Ryrie says that there are at least four words in the New Testament and Old Testament that fall under the category of God's love: his goodness, his mercy, his longsuffering, and his grace.

> Although distinctions are made, they are not exact. Goodness may be defined as God's benevolent concern for his creatures (Acts 14:17). Mercy is that aspect of His goodness that causes God to show pity and compassion (Eph. 2:4; James 5:11). Longsuffering speaks of self-restraint in the face of provocation (1 Pet. 3:20; 2 Pet. 3:15). Grace is the unmerited favor of God shown to man primarily in the person and work of Jesus Christ.[2]

Since God's love is filled with goodness, his continual concern finds ways to bring good into your life. Since God's love is merciful, anytime you're hurt, struggling, discouraged, or just having a bad day, God's love wants to step in and help you. He takes pity on you, hurts for you, and then he does something about it. And, since God's love is longsuffering and gracious, when you do bad things, stiff-arm God, or hurt other people, his love responds with the perfect mix of restraint, patience, and discipline.

Frankly, it's easier to ignore or doubt God's love than to dive into it. But we lose so much if we don't let him love us. He so desires for us to know his loving disposition that he went to extraordinary lengths to let us see it.

Five distinct implications of God's overwhelming love help me focus that love on the details of my life. Read the following phrases slowly as you ask God to confirm in your heart and mind that this is exactly how he thinks and feels toward you. After each phrase, ask yourself, "What would my life feel like and be like if I really believed God thinks of me this way?" Realize that this isn't how God thinks about a Billy

Graham or a Mother Teresa or the next person you run into today. It's how he thinks about *you*.

1. God's thoughts, intentions, desires, and plans are always for your good and never for your harm (Jer. 29:11; James 1:17).

You can trust his intentions. When God thinks of you, he thinks only about goodness and blessing—what he wants to give you and not how he wants to harm you. No matter how the immediate surroundings may look, God sees the big picture and has plans specially designed for your benefit.

2. God is kind, open, approachable, frank, and eager to be your friend (John 15:12–15).

He *wants* to be your friend. He longs to hear everything that you're going through and everything that's going on. He is the most loyal, attentive friend you could possibly have. Sometimes he just wants you to sit down and talk with him. He wants to share his life and his heart with you.

3. God emotionally identifies with your pain, joy, hopes, and dreams, and has chosen to allow your happiness to affect his own (John 11:33–36).

Although he is the infinite God of the universe, your pain causes him pain, your joy gives him a lift, your hopes bring excitement to his heart, and when there is tragedy in your life, he weeps with you—just as he wept with his friends at the death of Lazarus. It's an amazing thought that though the self-existing God needs no one, he has chosen to be so emotionally identified with your ups and downs, your dreams and hopes, that your happiness actually affects his. Scripture tells us we can actually grieve him. We can bring joy to his heart and we can bring sadness, because we matter that much to him.

4. He takes pleasure in you just for who you are completely apart from your performance and/or accomplishments (Ps. 139; Zeph. 3; Rom. 5:8).

Even if you had never done anything since you were born, God would take pleasure in you simply because of who you are. Think for a moment about someone who delights you—whose eyes you love gazing into, whose conversation you enjoy, whose company makes you happy. That's how God feels about you. He feels that way when you're obedient, godly, disciplined, and righteous, and he feels that way about you when you're irritable, sarcastic, selfish, and evil. In Zephaniah 3:17, God tells a rebellious people that he actually stands over them singing and rejoicing. The next time you feel like a failure, read that verse and enjoy the God who sings about you regardless of what you've done.

5. God is actively and creatively orchestrating people, circumstances, and events to express his affection and selective correction to provide for your highest good.

God is not way out there, unaware of and removed from your life, hoping things work out. He's not a clockmaker who wound the world up and is casually watching it wind down. He is carefully sovereign over every single event, from stoplights and phone calls to career opportunities and relationships. Every part of your life has been designed specifically to express his love, affection, and correction so you can have the best life possible.

When you consider God's love, how close are these five statements to your experience? Do you really think this is how God thinks and feels about you? If you're like most people, you may hesitate to claim his love. You may be thinking, "I wish God was like that and I hope he's like that, but how can I really believe he loves *me*?" God has revealed his loving intentions in a number of ways we can observe and examine.

How Does God Reveal His Love?

Before we look at the evidences of God's love, I want to pose a question: What more does God have to do to show you that he loves you? In other words, are you open to being persuaded about God's love? Or have you already decided that no evidence will ever convince you of it? At the very least, please look at the following six evidences of God's love with an open mind and heart.

Through Creation

God has revealed his love through creation. Genesis 1:26–27 describes the moment:

> Then God said, "Let us make man in our image, in our likeness, and let them rule over the fish of the sea and the birds of the air, over the livestock, over all the earth, and over all the creatures that move along the ground."

> So God created man in his own image,
>> in the image of God he created him;
>> male and female he created them.

The purpose behind God's creation of man and woman is to "rule over" the rest of creation. As the designated ruler, it makes sense to conclude that the actual ruler would design us to be like him in some way, or "in his image." We are like God because we represent him in creation. But there's more. Colossians 1:16 tells us, "For by him [Jesus] all things were created: things in heaven and on earth, visible and invisible, whether thrones or powers or rulers or authorities; all things were created by him and for him." Not only are we created *by* him in order to represent him; we are created *for* him—so he can relate to us in intimate love.

Have you ever watched an artist create a painting or listened to a musician write a song? Have you ever seen a group of people create a great idea and then develop a strategy to make it work? Have you ever watched the way a mother looks at a newborn baby, created through her and her husband? Our "creations" reveal a lot about us, just as all of creation shouts certain facts about God—his power, creativity, and other attributes. And in Genesis, we human beings are the pinnacle of God's creation; the way we were created tells us about his love.

Through Providence

God's providence—his general kindness to everyone—reveals his love. He bestows countless benefits on us every day, whether we acknowledge him or not. For example, think for a moment how many beats your heart has made today that you didn't have to consciously hope for. His providence is so faithful that we take it for granted.

The fact of God's unbiased providence troubles a lot of Christians. We may wonder whether or not God loves us, but we usually have a pretty good idea whom he *shouldn't* love. The fact that he loves people who are clearly sold out to evil provokes some of the same questions that make us doubt God's justice. Wouldn't we know God loves us if our enemies shrivel up and die? We have a hard time accepting the fact that God practices loving compassion to many people who frankly don't deserve it—including us. Do I mean that God loves Abu Bakr al-Baghdadi and the other leaders of ISIS? Absolutely. Kim Jong-un, Hitler, and Stalin too. And he also loves you and me.

Where do we get that? Look at Matthew 5:44–45: "But I tell you: Love your enemies and pray for those who persecute you, that you may be sons of your Father in heaven. He causes his sun to rise on the evil and the good, and sends rain on the righteous and the unrighteous." He tells us to love our enemies because that's what he is like! Paul develops the same point in Acts 17:24–27. He begins by acknowledging God as the Creator of all. He mentions the providence of God, who "gives all men life and breath and everything else." The "everything else" covers a lot—births, weddings, sunshine, joy, and the full range of human experience. Paul also emphasizes the common heritage of all humans: "From one man he made every nation of men" (v. 26). All of God's providence serves as his invitation to people to respond: "God did this so that men would seek him and perhaps reach out for him and find him, though he is not far from each one of us" (v. 27). Long before we believed, God did wonderful, kind, and good things every day in this world, causing rain to fall and crops to grow, and bringing joy to the hearts even of people who were evil. Most people who reflect on their lives before they became believers are amazed to find how many examples of God's outlandish love they can list. His providence draws us to him.

221

Through the Incarnation

God clearly revealed his love through the incarnation. The fact that he took on human flesh to pursue us in our own environment tells us volumes about his compassion. We'll look specifically at how the Son demonstrated the Father's love in a little while, but just the fact that God incarnated himself in human flesh makes a powerful statement about his love.

Jesus described God's purpose in the incarnation in Luke 19:10: "For the Son of Man came to seek and to save what was lost." Four chapters earlier, Jesus used three parables to illustrate the love of God. These parables were a response to the arrogant comments of religious leaders who were appalled that Jesus ate with sinners (Luke 15:2). Jesus described what happens when a loved sheep wanders away, when a valued coin is lost, and when a beloved son strays from home. God is like a shepherd who will cross a treacherous countryside to find a single lost sheep, and then celebrates with his friends when the sheep is found. He is like a woman who looks in every nook and cranny of the house to find a missing coin, and then calls up all the neighbors to tell them how she found it. He is like a father who is so thrilled to see his wayward son coming home that he ignores all past insults and injuries, runs recklessly out to meet his son, and throws a wild celebration over his return. The longing in God's heart to renew a broken relationship with us flows through these stories. He rejoices—not with a casual smile, but with singing and dancing—when we repent and turn to him.

Do you remember a time when you personally were pursued? Maybe in high school, some girl or some guy got interested in you and the word spread—Bob heard and told Mary, who told Jane, who told Phillip that she or he liked you. Or maybe you've had the experience of a coach recruiting you, or you've been asked to take a job because two or three people described you as competent and recommended you. Do you remember how good it felt to be pursued and wanted? That's what the incarnation was about—God pursuing *you*. The incarnation is a hint of how the God of infinite feelings feels about you. That's why he went to such great lengths to reach you.

Through Discipline

God also reveals his love when he chastens and protects us from self-destructive behavior. This is particularly true when we suffer the consequences of our actions. "The Lord disciplines those he loves, and he punishes everyone he accepts as a son" (Heb. 12:6). We almost instinctively suspect the love of a parent who ignores a misbehaving toddler. If a child is endangering his or her life, we expect parents not only to intervene but also to discipline and point out unacceptable behavior if they love their children. In today's American culture, we see that many parents view discipline as anti-loving and destructive to the child's ego. They will not step in to correct a toddler's misbehavior for fear of crushing the child's spirit. Those who do correct poor behavior are concerned about being reported to CPS. Discipline requires self-control, consistency, and presence.

One of the greatest evidences of love is when you care enough to confront, correct, and prevent those you love from self-destructive behaviors. God cares like that! You can be hardheaded like me, of course, and you can keep moving in the wrong direction. So he'll lean into you a little bit harder. But he always does it in love. He uses the appropriate discipline in the appropriate amounts to express his concern. Our hardships are proof of his love.

Through the Holy Spirit

The fifth revelation of God's love comes through the Holy Spirit. Our awareness of God's love will be a direct result of the work of God's Spirit in our lives. Romans 5:5 describes part of the process: "And hope does not disappoint us, because God has poured out his love into our hearts by the Holy Spirit, whom he has given us." The moment we trusted Christ as Lord and Savior, several events happened almost simultaneously: We were born again, sealed by the Spirit, adopted into God's family, and given a spiritual inheritance. Then the Spirit of God took up residence in us. The word *pour* here literally involves being tipped over, overflowing, and gushing out into our life. The Holy Spirit is like liquid pouring into us, filling us to overflowing—and the flavor of that liquid is love.

The Holy Spirit carries out several tasks in our lives.

> Those who are led by the Spirit of God are sons of God. For you did not receive a spirit that makes you a slave again to fear, but you received the Spirit of sonship. And by him we cry, "*Abba*, Father." The Spirit himself testifies with our spirit that we are God's children. Now if we are children, then we are heirs—heirs of God and co-heirs with Christ, if indeed we share in his sufferings in order that we may also share in his glory. (Rom. 8:14–17)

The Spirit is working when you read God's Word and sense his voice speaking to you from the pages. The Spirit is acting when you're discouraged and you get a timely phone call from a concerned member of the body of Christ. Through the Holy Spirit, God pours out his love in your heart so you can experience it intimately. The Spirit is present when you feel relaxed and loved in God's presence and find yourself calling him a name as familiar as "Dad."

Through His Son

As with every attribute, God's ultimate expression of love did not come in words; it came in a person: Jesus. That's a crucial point to make because there's such a huge gap between the way that God longs to be seen and the way he is actually seen. A lot of people believe in God but reject Jesus. In order to do that, they have to redefine God, and they worship a figment of their own imagination. How do we know? Because according to the Bible, Jesus is the exact representation and fullness of God (Heb. 1:3; Col. 1:19). Jesus is how God defined himself. No one can accept God while rejecting Jesus. If we really want to see him with 20/20 vision—in other words, if we are ever going to see God as he really longs to be seen—we have to embrace God incarnate. God is invisible, and people can (and do) speculate widely about what he's like. But Jesus is visible. We can *see* all of God's attributes, including his love, in him. Jesus demonstrated the reality of God's love by coming to the world, and he revealed the nature of that love by the way he lived.

Jesus modeled God's love. Jesus touched the untouchables, spoke to the forsaken, and reached the unreachable. In retrospect, the disciples remembered seeing Jesus love everyone. But in the warm fellowship of Jesus's presence, the disciples seemed too immersed in Jesus's love to appreciate what it meant. One of the most frustrating moments for Jesus came during the Last Supper. Moments after he "showed them the full extent of his love" (John 13:1) by putting on a towel and washing their feet, the disciples showed their lack of understanding. First, Thomas admitted he didn't see the point of it all (John 14:5–7). Then Philip said, "Lord, show us the Father and that will be enough for us" (v. 8). I can imagine this being one of those moments when Jesus felt like pulling his hair out. The disappointment and longing in his words is telling: "Don't you know me, Philip, even after I have been among you such a long time? Anyone who has seen me has seen the Father.

How can you say, 'Show us the Father'?" (John 14:9). In other words, "What is it about this you don't get?! When you've seen how I respond to a prostitute, a leper, or the sick and hungry, *you've seen the Father!*"

When you and I want to know what God is like, all we have to do is look at Jesus. He has modeled the passion and the grace and the truth of the Father himself.

Jesus's teaching revealed God's love. A few pages back, we talked about Luke 15 and the three parables about God's love. Those stories are examples of God's pursuing love. They are also examples of God's unconditional love. Take a moment to read Luke 15 for yourself and let Jesus's words about God's love soak into your heart. The story of the lost son reverberates with unconditional love, releasing a son intent on going his own way, faithfully waiting for that son while he strays, and then joyfully welcoming that son when he returns. Does God love us when we are good and nice, clean and spiffy, tithing and praying, avoiding bad thoughts, and managing not to "lose it" in weeks? Of course he does! But that's not why. These stories tell us that he loves us when we get lost, when we squander all he's given us, when we reject him, when we run away, when we get involved in immorality, when we hurt other people, when we're sarcastic, and when we are completely self-focused. His love doesn't casually overlook these things; we need to repent of our sins to experience it. But the love is always there. It's unconditional.

The Father is searching every day, waiting for us to come home. Our repentance doesn't generate the love he has for us; it brings us into an experience of his love. Jesus taught that the Father feels compassion for you every single moment of every single day. His arms are open and he's going to kill the fatted calf and put a ring on your finger and sandals on your feet to let you know you're a beloved daughter or son. He's got a warm coat of blessings to put over your shoulders when you step in from the cold. He wants to show you how much he has loved you all along.

Jesus demonstrated on the cross the depth of God's love. First John 3:16 says, "This is how we know what love is: Jesus Christ laid down his life for us. And we ought to lay down our lives for our brothers." If someone asks you how you know God loves you, there's no better answer than this one: Because Jesus died for me. God's Word even says it this way in Romans 5:8: "But God demonstrates his own love for us in this: While we were still sinners, Christ died for us." Because we were sinners, we needed a demonstration. In spite of our sinfulness, God gave it to us by sending Christ to die for us. God doesn't love us because we are good. When we were still hostile to him, Jesus died on the cross to pay for our sin and to demonstrate the full extent of his love.

An object's value is always determined by the price paid for it. The item on an auction block might look like a worthless piece of wood to some, a potential wall decoration to another, or an inexpensive instrument for a beginning violin student to another. But the one who realizes that the violin was crafted by Stradivarius will bid a seemingly exorbitant amount. Why? Because to that person, it's worth a lot. Its value correlates to the price paid for it. The value of God's payment for us tells us how much we are worth to him. We are worth the life of his Son.

In 2002, a drawing was discovered in what used to be a maid's room in one of the Smithsonian's museums. The chalk drawing of a candelabra was one of five drawings sold collectively to the museum in 1940 for $60. For decades, it sat in storage until one day a visiting scholar recognized it for what it was: an original Michelangelo. Today, it is valued at more than $12 million.

What was the difference between the drawing in 2002 and the drawing now? Nothing. It's the same drawing it has always been. The only difference is that the artist is now known and demand for it is high. It is highly valued because there are numerous collectors who would pay millions for it.

Maybe you've felt like a humble sketch stashed away unnoticed in a storage room. The cross should convince you otherwise. In his sacrifice, Jesus clearly claimed you as his own. The artist has been revealed and the demand for your redemption is high. The crucifixion is the evidence of love: there's a Collector—in this case the Artist himself—who was willing to pay an enormous price for his beloved work of art.

The Question

Earlier I said I would come back to this question: *What more does God have to do to show you that he loves you?* I meet people all the time who have never seriously looked at the evidence but are convinced God doesn't love them. They have come to the wrong conclusion because they assume God's love operates the same way ours does—conditionally. Even people who have tasted God's love often revert to spinning their wheels to prove that they are worthy. We try to use the same tactic with God that we use with others—we hide, protect, manipulate, and image-cast in order to let everyone know that we are a little better than we really are. I know because I've seen it in my own life.

People who try to demonstrate to God that they are worthy of his love are eventually going to have a major problem with stress. I know, because it's human nature and we've all done that. But a person who allows God's grace to transform him or her from the inside can just relax and be loved. God's grace is his unmerited love and compassion for us. When we really believe that we are loved and accepted, we no longer have to be the best, to compare ourselves to others, to strive to make a good impression, to compete for attention, or to run around looking for love in all the wrong places. And if you think about it, those games we play are the source of the vast majority of our anxieties.

When I finally realized that the eternal God of the universe has a holy pleasure when he looks at me, that he doesn't want to harm me but to do good for me—and that his opinion of me is not contingent on anything I do—it revolutionized my life. And he gives every one of us the same promise: his love is unconditional, it's free, and all we have to do to experience it is accept it and rejoice in it. That truth will set you absolutely free, and then you'll be free to love people instead of play games with them to get them to love you. It's time for us to stop trying to earn God's love and let ourselves experience it. It's time to stop coming up with ways to deserve his love and learn to respond to the love he has already clearly shown us.

How Do We Respond to the Love of God?

Once we realize that God has done more than enough to demonstrate his love, the next move is ours. God has said, "I love you" in countless ways. How do we say it back to him? How do we respond to his love?

We Must Receive

First, we receive his love into our hearts by faith. Too often we read a verse like John 3:16 as if we are reading a generic Valentine's card in the store. We need to realize the card has already been delivered and it has our name on it. If you plug your name into it—not just "God so loved the world," but "God loved *you*"—you'll begin to understand the personal message in it. You'll realize God gave his Son *for you* so that eternal life might be *yours*.

God's love has been delivered, but too often the card lies unopened, or opened but not really read, or read once and not reviewed very often. Jesus is God's living expression of love, willing to walk every moment of every day with us, continually reassuring us of God's love. If God's promise of love has always been like a card mailed to someone else, stop right now and receive it as if it had your name on it—because it does.

We Must Believe

The next step in responding to God's love is not only to receive it, but to believe it. By faith, we can take his love to heart. The receiving happens in a moment; the believing goes on for a lifetime. In 1 John 4:13–16, the old apostle John is writing to those who have already received Christ.

> We know that we live in him and he in us, because he has given us of his Spirit. And we have seen and testify that the Father has sent his Son to be the Savior of the world. If anyone acknowledges that Jesus is the Son of God, God lives in him and he in God. And so we know and rely on the love God has for us.
>
> God is love. Whoever lives in love lives in God, and God in him.

John's summary statement says that we "know and rely on the love God has for us." We experience his love, feel it, understand it, depend on it, trust in it, rest in it, and live by it. God's love repeatedly travels back and forth on the eighteen-inch trip between heart and mind. The journey is marked with moments of loving God back with everything we've got.

Relying on God's love is not about performance, not about earning our keep, and not about getting brownie points. The Christian life involves understanding his love and letting it transform us into loving people. It's not about religion, rules, or doing; it's about a relation ship with the eternal God, by the power of the Holy Spirit, who takes the redemptive work of Jesus Christ and births new life in us. Out of that relationship, transformation occurs, and it affects everything! But the changes are by-products of—not conditions for—his love in our hearts.

How can we get that from our head down to our heart and back again? We practice "knowing" and "relying" in at least three different ways:

1. SATURATE YOUR MIND WITH THE TRUTH OF GOD'S LOVE FOR US.

Consider the remarkable character of God's love as seen in Scriptures like Romans 8:38–39:

> For I am convinced that neither death nor life, neither angels nor demons, neither the present nor the future, nor any powers, neither height nor depth, nor anything else in all creation, will be able to separate us from the love of God that is in Christ Jesus our Lord.

God wants us to know that nothing—not even our own junk—can separate us from his love.

Soak your mind in that truth and others. Let John remind you, "How great is the love the Father has lavished on us, that we should be called children of God! And that is what we are!" (1 John 3:1). Saturate your mind in the reality that you're loved.

2. Ask God to help you grasp his love.

Memorize Paul's prayer for the Ephesians and pray it for the people in your life. Include yourself in the prayer:

> When I think of the wisdom and scope of God's plan, I fall to my knees and pray to the Father, the Creator of everything in heaven and on earth. I pray that from his glorious, unlimited resources he will give you mighty inner strength through his Holy Spirit. And I pray that Christ will be more and more at home in your hearts as you trust in him. May your roots go down deep into the soil of God's marvelous love. And may you have the power to understand, as all God's people should, how wide, how long, how high, and how deep his love really is. May you experience the love of Christ, though it is so great you will never fully understand it. Then you will be filled with the fullness of life and power that comes from God. (Eph. 3:14–19 NLT)

Ask God to apply this prayer to your life and he will. It's a prayer that the God of love could not refuse to answer.

3. Refuse to seek love in cheap substitutes.

One of the easiest mistakes to make is looking for love in the wrong places. Our craving for love leads us to many false, unworthy substitutes. God's Word warns us of such futile efforts in 1 John 2:15–16:

> Do not love the world or anything in the world. If anyone loves the world, the love of the Father is not in him. For everything in the world—the cravings of sinful man, the lust of his eyes and the boasting of what he has and does—comes not from the Father but from the world.

God knows why we're so drawn to the bigger houses, stuff, and toys. He understands why we're drawn to visual sexual images. He recognizes why we want everyone to think we're so cool, strong, and smart. We think if we had the right possessions, skills, or looks, then we would be loved, affirmed, and valued.

But "the world and anything in the world" are just cheap substitutes, and that's why God warns us not to love them. We can enjoy them as good gifts, but we are not to love them. They can remind us of the Giver, but should never become a substitute for him. They will never be able to love us the way we desperately want to be loved. Only our Creator can love us that way.

We Must Give It Away

The best way we know we have received and believe God's love for us is when we begin bestowing God's love, giving it away to others. Trying to hoard it for ourselves is a fruitless effort and demonstrates that we still don't understand it. The more of God's love we give away, the more he supplies. It's the ultimate gift that keeps on giving.

God's Word tells us that bestowing his love on others is an act of our will, by faith. We really believe God's love is inexhaustible when we try our best to give it away. If we really think there's enough to go around, we won't try to keep it to ourselves. Giving it away is a command. It was one of Jesus's last instructions to his disciples: "A new command I give you: Love one another. As I have loved you, so you must love one another" (John 13:34). This isn't just a nice request to feel good about others, it's a command to love *as he did*—sacrificially. The ultimate test that we are Jesus's disciples is whether or not we love each other (John 13:35).

John makes it a special point to remind us that the command to love is also a calling.

> This is how we know what love is: Jesus Christ laid down his life for us.
> And we ought to lay down our lives for our brothers. If anyone has ma-
> terial possessions and sees his brother in need but has no pity on him,
> how can the love of God be in him? Dear children, let us not love with
> words or tongue but with actions and in truth. (1 John 3:16–18)

John was not talking about ooey-gooey sentimentalism. He was describing a radical love that costs. This kind of love notices a need and gives
sacrificially to meet it. This love sees a hurt and steps in. If the need
involves money, love gives money. If the need requires time, love gives
time. If someone needs to hear about Christ, love shares faith.

Terms like "command" and "calling" sometimes make us fear that bestowing God's love on others sounds too one-sided. But God promises
that he will make love worthwhile. One of my favorite biblical promises
is found in Luke 6:38, where Jesus says, "Give, and it will be given to
you. A good measure, pressed down, shaken together and running over,
will be poured into your lap. For with the measure you use, it will be
measured to you." As we've already seen, love can't be hoarded. God's
love is dynamic and flowing. Giving it away never exhausts it. The returns
we experience correspond with the investments we make. If we lavish
a teaspoonful of love on others, we're going to get a teaspoonful back.
If we continually fill a tanker load from the ocean of God's love and
provide a constant flow into the lives of others, we will be overwhelmed
by the love of God pouring back into our lives.

That doesn't mean that enjoying and bestowing God's love makes everything else easy. God never promises that. It means that it will be
fulfilling. In the midst of hurt, pain, and struggle in a fallen world, you
will have a deep sense of significance and affirmation, being eternally
valued and accepted. You will experience God's love.

My Experience with the Love of God

It had been a stressful month for our family. Theresa and I had both been running on empty and felt like we just couldn't keep going. We were looking forward to Thanksgiving, with all of the family getting together just to relax and enjoy each other for a couple of days. But on Thursday morning, we got a call from Theresa's mother's doctor, who told us she had congestive heart failure, was very weak, and if we wanted to see her we needed to come right away.

Our day of refreshing vanished. It was like getting to the last mile of a marathon and being told there's another mile to go. So instead of relaxing, we spent Thanksgiving getting plane tickets for Theresa and her sister and working through all sorts of issues. I got really low.

Saturday morning I went to my favorite donut store like I usually do to review my Sunday message. But I wasn't in the mood to pray, to read my Bible, or even to get ready to preach. That's not a good sign on a Saturday morning, but it was reality. *Obedience isn't a feeling*, I told myself. So I wrote a few things in my journal, tried to pray a little, and told God I needed to experience his love. Then I read a couple of chapters of my Bible. Nothing dramatic there. Then I read a little devotional Theresa had given me. It had a phrase that started playing over and over again in my mind: "the God of all comfort." I pulled out my journal again and wrote, "If you're really the God of all comfort, will you comfort me today?"

I started to review my notes for my message, and one of my closest friends walked in. We sat there for forty-five minutes while I poured out my heart and he just listened and loved me. It didn't even occur to me that there might have been a connection between my prayer and my friend showing up.

A little later, another friend called, and even though I didn't say very much, he knew me well enough to detect the discouragement in my voice. "Tell me what's going on," he said.

So I told him I wasn't doing very well, we talked for half an hour, and I still didn't realize God had showed up.

I got home and my son asked me how I was doing. "Not very well, Ryan," I told him. "I'm discouraged and just can't get out of this funk."

"Do you want to pray?" he asked.

Honestly, I wasn't in the mood, but when you've raised a child to respond that way, what can you say? So I agreed, of course, and this twenty-one-year-old kid really prayed his heart out for me.

Then I found a note on the table that one of my friends had called just to say hello. I called him back, but couldn't talk long since I was about to drive my daughter Annie somewhere. He asked if he could ride along. On the way back, we stopped in a coffee shop and talked for an hour, and he just listened and loved me.

I got home again and shot some baskets with Ryan, and we ended up having one of those talks that you always dream about as a dad.

Do you see a pattern? It took me until about the fourth person, but I finally saw it too. The love of God is real, and the Spirit of God will be poured out into your heart and prompt you to cry out to your Father. And at your deepest times of need, when you feel most unlovable, worthless, and weak, his grace will show up.

God's love for me was there, even when I didn't feel it. It had been there all along, and through his Word, a devotional, and a succession of people who cared, he showed it to me.

He longs to show all of us, even in our times of deepest need. *Especially* in our times of deepest need. All he asks is that we open our eyes and see it, and then live in the reality of his infinite love.

Live It Out—B.I.O.

"Bio" is a word that is synonymous with "life." Found in those three simple letters, B.I.O. is the key to helping you become the person God wants you to be.

B *Come BEFORE God daily.* Meet with him personally through his Word and prayer to enjoy his presence, receive his direction, and follow his will.

I *Do Life IN COMMUNITY weekly.* Structure your week to personally connect in safe relationships that provide love, support, transparency, challenge, and accountability.

O *ON MISSION 24/7.* Cultivate a mindset to "live out" Jesus's love for others through acts of sacrifice and service at home, work, play, and church.

Come BEFORE God

- Write the following definition on a notecard, smartphone, or tablet and place it where you will read it when you get up in the morning and when you go to bed. Don't try to memorize it. Simply read it in a spirit of prayer and let the reality of God's love pour over your soul.

God's love is his holy disposition toward all that he has created that compels him to express unconditional affection and selective correction to provide the highest quality of existence, both now and forever, for the object of his love.

- Near the definition, write Romans 8:38–39 and meditate on that thought. Each time you read it, begin by asking, "What would it be like if I really believed that God loves me regardless of what I have or have not done? How would that change how I see myself and how I relate to others?"

  I am convinced that neither death nor life, neither angels nor demons, neither the present nor the future, nor any powers, neither height nor depth, nor anything else in all creation, will be able to separate us from the love of God that is in Christ Jesus our Lord. (Rom. 8:38–39)

- Join me in making the following prayer your own for the next seven days:

  O Lord, the God who is love, as I consider the infinite nature of your compassion, mercy, and favor, grant that I might

  - *grasp and accept the reality of your love,*

  - *abandon all the things I've tried to use as substitutes, and*

  - *sacrificially demonstrate your love to others.*

  Let me rely on and rest in the certainty of your unconditional love, even when I don't feel it. Help me to see it even in difficult times, to know that it's always there regardless of my performance, and to thank you for it constantly. Let it really sink into my heart as I've never known it before. In Jesus's name, Amen.

- Think about a time when you felt deeply loved by God. Why?

- In what ways have you sought a "cheap substitute" for God's love? Why?

- Ask for God's help in letting the truth of his love permeate your heart.

Do Life IN Community

- Write a letter, card, or email blessing to a friend who has shown you true, authentic love. Tell them what their friendship has meant to you and the impact they have made in your life.

Be ON Mission

- Go out of your way to love someone in your world who is hard to love and ask God to give you a heart for loving that person unconditionally.

10

THE FAITHFULNESS OF GOD

Because of the LORD's great love we are not consumed,
    for his compassions never fail.
They are new every morning;
    great is your faithfulness.

Lamentations 3:22–23

The desolation of the city is so complete that witnesses find it hard to blame human destructiveness. Maybe an earthquake would better explain the chaos. Clearly, God's anger has been unleashed. Large buildings and massive walls have been toppled and scattered like toy blocks. Streets are filled with evidence of hurried and unsuccessful departure; bodies lie drying in the sun. The scavengers have already had their fill.

A broken man, pacing in the dimness of a dusty room, dictates his words to another who sits with pen in hand. There is bitter devastation in his voice; his lament is filled with pain. He sobs and groans as he voices the anguish of his heart. His audience is the handful who escaped the destruction. His subject is God.

Pausing for a moment, his grief over the city turns inward:

> I'm the man who has seen trouble,
>> trouble coming from the lash of GOD's anger.
> He took me by the hand and walked me
>> into pitch-black darkness.
> Yes, he's given me the back of his hand
>> over and over and over again.
>
> He turned me into a scarecrow
>> of skin and bones, then broke the bones.
> He hemmed me in, ganged up on me,
>> poured on the trouble and hard times.
> He locked me up in deep darkness,
>> like a corpse nailed inside a coffin.
>
> He shuts me in so I'll never get out,
>> manacles my hands, shackles my feet.
> Even when I cry out and plead for help,
>> he locks up my prayers and throws away the key.
> He sets up blockades with quarried limestone.
>> He's got me cornered.
>
> He's a prowling bear tracking me down,
>> a lion in hiding ready to pounce.
> He knocked me from the path and ripped me to pieces.
>> When he finished, there was nothing left of me.
> He took out his bow and arrows
>> and used me for target practice.
>
> He shot me in the stomach
>> with arrows from his quiver.

Everyone took me for a joke,
> made me the butt of their mocking ballads.

He forced rotten, stinking food down my throat,
> bloated me with vile drinks.

He ground my face into the gravel.
> He pounded me into the mud.

I gave up on life altogether.
> I've forgotten what the good life is like.

I said to myself, "This is it. I'm finished.
> God is a lost cause."

I'll never forget the trouble, the utter lostness,
> the taste of ashes, the poison I've swallowed.

I remember it all—oh, how well I remember—
> the feeling of hitting the bottom. (Lam. 3:1–20 Message)

What a picture of disillusionment! Have you ever felt that low? Did you identify with some of the words in that eloquent lament? Maybe you thought, "I can relate. I've felt like God is against me. I've been depressed about life and I've had my face rubbed in it. I know the taste of gravel and ashes. I've wondered if God is a lost cause."

You may be surprised to learn that the passage above comes from the heart of the Bible, penned by one of God's prophets, Jeremiah. When it came to talking to God and about God, Jeremiah didn't believe in holding anything back. When he had something on his mind, he unloaded it completely. He dumped on God like few other people in history—and lived to tell about it.

We might think a passage like this was written by someone who no longer cared what God thought or who was prepared to suffer divine wrath. But though Jeremiah, "the weeping prophet," lived a long and mournful life, he never lost sight of God's faithfulness. Regardless of

243

the immediate circumstances, his confidence in God was unshakeable. The passage above is simply one of many in which Jeremiah pours out every last drop of anger, sorrow, and shock. Still, there's a glimpse of hope:

> But there's one other thing I remember,
>   and remembering, I keep a grip on hope:
>
> GOD's loyal love couldn't have run out,
>   his merciful love couldn't have dried up.
>
> They're created new every morning.
>   How great your faithfulness! (Lam. 3:21–23 Message)

What helps us "keep a grip on hope"? Do we, like Jeremiah, freely voice all our feelings to God, clearing the air so we can focus on his agenda in our difficulties? Or do we conclude that our feelings of despair and sadness accurately reflect ultimate reality? It depends on the object of our hope. In fact, the grinding hardships of life do us a great service, in spite of how much we dislike them. Difficulties reveal what kind of hope we have.

Oxygen of the Soul

Before we look at God's faithfulness, let me begin by making three observations about the role of hope in our lives:

- *We all depend on something or someone to "hold us up" inside.*

  All human beings depend on something or someone to make us feel significant and to keep us going—even if it's just ourselves. Whether you are a believer or unbeliever, you are counting on something or someone to support your life and provide significance. That someone or something is your hope.

- *When that something or someone is "coming through for us," we experience a sense of peace, satisfaction, and optimism about the future.*

Hope takes on an amazing variety of forms. People find hope in sports, success, money, family, beauty, and ability, to mention a few. When things are clicking and life is going well in the area of your hopes, you feel peaceful and optimistic. You say, "Life is good!" But we experience wide swings between contentment and disappointment because what we place our hopes on often doesn't prove dependable.

- *When that something or someone "fails to come through for us" we experience a sense of anxiety, dissatisfaction, and ultimately despair.*

Hope can vanish in a heartbeat. When a pro athlete has a career-ending injury, hope based on ability proves empty. Or when a biopsy report comes back positive, and three weeks later you bury someone you dearly love, hope based on health proves futile. When your hopes are in your job and suddenly you don't have one because the economy turned sour, hope vanishes. If whatever holds you up—a thing, a person, or a plan—for whatever reason doesn't come through, your sense of peace and satisfaction is gone. Instead, you experience anxiety, concern, and despair.

Someone has said that hope is the oxygen of the soul. We can live for weeks without food and survive days without water. But without oxygen, we are only minutes from death. If hope is oxygen for the soul, we can't live long without it. When what we're really hoping in is gone, we die.

Most of us don't like to think about what we are depending on because when we do, we usually have to admit our hopes are temporary and less than reliable. The instability of everything around us makes us anxious. Wouldn't it make sense, if possible, to find something or someone that would always come through for us in any situation?

That would be a great deal. The question is, where do you find that kind of person, or that kind of hope? What do you do when it seems like life isn't worth living, when whatever is holding you up suddenly gets pulled out from under you?

Jeremiah had an answer. He left us written proof of how bad things got, yet also how hope prevailed. If we want to face life with the kind of honesty and hope that we find in Jeremiah, then, like him, we've got to discover the faithfulness of God.

God's faithfulness offers hope for every person, no matter what's going on in your life and how bad it is right now—stress, health problems, financial problems, marital problems, problems with your children, loneliness, desperately wanting to be married, desperately wishing you weren't, or any other issue you might have. Wherever you are and whatever pain you are in, God's loving compassion toward you will never, ever end. If you are feeling helpless and hopeless, the answer is his faithfulness. And if you are feeling unbeatable and successful today because of something other than God's faithfulness, your happiness is temporary.

The secret to a life of unending joy and peace involves finding something or someone who will "come through" for you 100 percent of the time in any and every situation forever. So let's discover together that "someone" who promises to come through for you always in every situation—the eternal, unchanging, faithful God of the universe.

The secret to a life of unending joy and peace involves finding something or someone who will "come through" for you 100 percent of the time in any and every situation forever.

Defining God's Faithfulness

Dictionaries define *faithfulness* as steadfast in affection or allegiance. In other words, someone faithful is loyal, dependable, and firm in adhering to promises or observing duty.

When a person who has proven faithful says something, we know it's binding, true to the facts, and up to a standard. It's constant. We can imagine faithfulness for years or sometimes even decades—and even then, there are occasional lapses. But we have to remember that God is not like us. When the Bible speaks of his faithfulness, it speaks in terms of eternity and perfection. If we apply our definition of faithfulness to God, we realize that he is dependable, trustworthy, loyal, staunch, resolute, constant, reliable, and true to his word—always and forever. When he speaks to you from Scripture, you can take it to the bank.

God's Word is true regardless of any circumstantial evidence to the contrary. He keeps his promises, he's consistent with his character, and he will come through for you 100 percent of the time. In fact, God's faithfulness applies to everything else about him. It shines through all his other attributes. Tozer writes,

Quick Definition

All of God's acts are consistent with all of His attributes. No attribute contradicts any other, but all harmonize and blend into each other in the infinite abyss of the Godhead. . . . God, being who He is, cannot cease to be what He is. . . . He is at once faithful and immutable, so all His words and acts must be and must remain faithful.[1]

Ultimately, we need to see all the attributes working together. If we do not understand and trust God's faithfulness, we will not trust the rest of his character either. When we hurt, we need to know that God is faithful. We always need to count on that, whether circumstances are going uphill, downhill, or have even hit rock bottom. We need to be firmly grounded in the fact of his faithfulness. His character does not depend on our emotions, thought, or rapidly changing events. Apart from God, everything is changeable, passing, and unworthy of our hope. God is different. He is unwavering, and he welcomes our trust.

God is faithful to his Word, to his promises, to his people, and to his character because he cannot be otherwise. You can depend on him 100 percent of the time. He will never let you down. He may not do what you want him to do exactly when you want him to or even how you want him to. He may not orchestrate it in a way that you can understand it now, or perhaps ever. But he will *never* let you down.

How Does God Reveal His Faithfulness?

Just as all the attributes of God flow from a consistent character, they are also revealed in consistent ways. The same ways God has used to reveal his goodness, sovereignty, holiness, wisdom, and other attributes can also tell us about his faithfulness.

Through His Creation

God reveals himself through creation. God's Word is filled with exclamations like Psalm 119:90: "Your faithfulness continues through all generations; you established the earth, and it endures." Or Psalm 145:13–16:

> Your kingdom is an everlasting kingdom,
>> and your dominion endures through all generations.
>
> The LORD is faithful to all his promises
>> and loving toward all he has made.
> The LORD upholds all those who fall
>> and lifts up all who are bowed down.
> The eyes of all look to you,
>> and you give them their food at the proper time.
> You open your hand
>> and satisfy the desires of every living thing.

Creation demonstrates God is faithful. He has fixed the planets and balanced the solar system. We discover far-flung galaxies and give them names, but they were there all along, carefully placed by our heavenly Father in their exact location.

The precision of creation is illustrated by ancient civilizations. Structures like ziggurats and temples were often positioned by the astronomical observations of their builders. We can still see the results: at certain intervals, often measured in years, these structures cast shadows, display the alignment of stars, or demonstrate some other universal rule. If the tilt of the earth were off by just a little, not only would these kinds of architectural tributes to an exact Creator be impossible, the world itself would be a hostile place—the north pole would be hot, the equator would be cold, and we'd all be dead.

God has demonstrated through creation that only in rare times does he circumvent the "laws" of nature. Science exists not because physical laws have a personality of their own, but because the Person behind them has put them in place and runs them with remarkable, observable regularity and precision. *That's* faithfulness. We see consistency in nature because the God of the universe is utterly consistent. The result is a creation full of laws—gravity, the speed of light, thermodynamics, and the like—that you can bank on. The cause (God) created the effect (creation) to reflect his character. He longs to be seen in his creative glory!

Through His People

Second, God has revealed his faithfulness through his dealings with his people. The biblical story of the chosen descendants of a chosen man named Abraham is a shining testament to God's faithfulness. It is also a sad record of the offenses that people commit in spite of his goodness. God kept his promises, followed through on his warnings, and persevered in his plan to use a nation to bless the world. The promise God made to Abraham in Genesis 12:1–3 has not been broken to this day.

Numerous Old Testament passages illustrate God's ongoing faithfulness to his people. "You will be true to Jacob, and show mercy to Abraham," Micah 7:20 affirms. "The LORD swore an oath to David, a sure oath that he will not revoke," Psalm 132:11 pledges. His faithfulness is clearly seen in Israel, and it carries seamlessly over into the church. When Jesus said, "And I tell you that you are Peter, and on this rock I will build my church, and the gates of Hades will not overcome it" (Matt. 16:18), he included two promises related to God's faithfulness: he committed himself to *building* his church and to *preserving* it. God has steadfastly fulfilled these promises in a frequently hostile environment. Whether opposition has come through attempts to wipe out Israel or to destroy the church, God has proven faithful.

I love to hear believers talk about the way God has demonstrated his faithfulness in their lives. The stories are amazing and heartwarming. God overcomes obstacles, does miracles, opens doors, and comes through in ways that go above and beyond our wildest expectations. God is sometimes embarrassingly obvious in his lavish commitment to his promises.

In 2009, the Living on the Edge radio broadcast was heard on over nine hundred stations in America with morning time slots in the top ten cities. The teaching ministry continued to expand, but I became increasingly burdened by the growing number of Christians who listen to God's Word but are not experiencing transformation in their lives. Jesus's command was to make disciples, not simply teach his Word to millions of people across the country.

In a moment of truth and honest evaluation we voluntarily left three of the top ten cities in order to use the financial resources to create small group materials focused on discipleship. The move was not well received by the Christian radio industry, and we had no previous experience or guarantee of success with creating small group materials. We were holding to the promise that God would be faithful if we would align ourselves with his top priority and our clear calling—discipleship.

After creating our first small group resource, we told our listening audience that if they would commit to going through the small group resource with their family, small group, or Sunday school class we would send it to them for free. Not a great business model, but it is how God led us to begin.

Seven thousand people responded and started small groups all across the country. We had already paid for the development of the small group resource, but the hard costs to produce the materials and ship them was about $22,600. About thirty days later our accounting staff member stopped by my office and said, "I have something I think you'd like to see. We didn't ask anyone for any money and yet 377 people spontaneously gave to help cover the costs—many of them writing to say they realized someone has to pay for this and they want to help. Of the 377 gifts, 100 of them were over $100." Finally she said, "Our total income spontaneously given with no request was $23,196." God is faithful!

Since that time we have developed over twenty-five small group resources, launched over 300,000 small groups, and seen over 3.5 million people participate in America and around the world.

We are still thrilled to teach God's Word via radio, television, podcast, and through our mobile app, but these small group resources have become a means to help people not only hear the Word but begin the discipleship journey for themselves.

Through His Spirit

Not only does God keep his promises externally, on the stage of history, he is also faithful internally. He demonstrates his reliability through his Spirit, maintaining his promises in ways that are not as obvious, but that yield life-changing results. Jesus promised,

> If you love me, you will obey what I command. And I will ask the Father, and he will give you another Counselor to be with you forever—the Spirit of truth. The world cannot accept him, because it neither sees him nor knows him. But you know him, for he lives with you and will be in you. I will not leave you as orphans; I will come to you. (John 14:15–18)

Our ability to obey Christ's commands depends on our willingness to rely on the Spirit's power in our lives, every moment of every day. The presence and work of God's Spirit produce certain results, some of which are listed in Galatians 5:22–23: "The fruit of the Spirit is love, joy, peace, patience, kindness, goodness, faithfulness, gentleness and self-control. Against such things there is no law." God exhibits his faithfulness by the ministry of the Holy Spirit producing those characteristics in us.

Through His Character

God reveals his faithfulness through his character. When it comes to the issue of faithfulness, God makes it clear that his reputation is at stake. The honor of his name is on the line. Regardless of our shaky experiences with anyone else, God longs for us to have complete confidence in his integrity. "God is not a man, that he should lie, nor a son of man, that he should change his mind. Does he speak and then not act? Does he promise and not fulfill?" (Num. 23:19). This was Isaiah's insight: "O LORD, you are my God; I will exalt you and praise your name, for in perfect faithfulness you have done marvelous things, things planned long ago" (Isa. 25:1). The Twenty-third Psalm underlines God's motivation: "He guides me in paths of righteousness *for his name's sake*" (v. 3, emphasis added). Anytime God's name is mentioned in Scripture, it ought to make us think of his perfect character and sterling reputation. He is utterly trustworthy and unwaveringly steadfast. His name represents his perfection.

Through His Word

Because God's character is faithful, the statements he makes are always true. That applies not only to his words but to his actions. The Bible is the record of God's complete reliability. Not only does the Word say he simply *cannot* lie (Titus 1:2; Heb. 6:18), it proves it. The Bible is a lengthy demonstration of God's perfect track record.

One of the clearest statements of the faithfulness of his Word is in Isaiah:

> As the rain and the snow
>   come down from heaven,
> and do not return to it
>   without watering the earth
> and making it bud and flourish,
>   so that it yields seed for the sower and bread for the eater,
> so is my word that goes out from my mouth:
>   It will not return to me empty
> but will accomplish what I desire
>   and achieve the purpose for which I sent it. (Isa. 55:10–11)

Where God's Word falls, crops grow. When we take in God's Word like the soil absorbs rain, God tells us we can count on good results. When Jesus prayed for us in John 17, he made it a point to emphasize the importance of God's Word in our lives. "Sanctify them by the truth; your word is truth" (John 17:17). Jesus was asking his Father to "sanctify them"—make them (and us) holy. "Make these followers of mine followers of yours by your word. Your word is truth," he prayed. When God's Word makes an impact on our lives, we become part of the demonstration of his faithfulness.

God reveals his faithfulness through his truthfulness in his covenants (Deut. 7:9), his promises (Heb. 10:23), and his prophecies. He never breaks a covenant or a promise. They are rock-solid guarantees, more certain than money in the bank. And his predictions never fail; they always—without exception—take place.

This record of predicting the future is one of the distinctive qualities of Christianity. His prophecies are never guesses—he always knows.

> I am the LORD; that is my name!
>> I will not give my glory to another
>> or my praise to idols.
> See, the former things have taken place,
>> and new things I declare;
> before they spring into being
>> I announce them to you. (Isa. 42:8–9)

God gave us hundreds of prophecies—about the Messiah, about specific historical developments, about Israel, about the future. Some of them were written hundreds of years before the fact, and yet every one that has come to pass has been fulfilled to the very details. Not a single one of God's prophecies has failed. The ones that have not yet been fulfilled are just as certain. We can count on them because he is faithful.

Through His Son

As with each of God's attributes, the ultimate example of God's faithfulness comes to us through his Son. Isaiah 11:5 describes the Messiah: "Righteousness will be his belt and faithfulness the sash around his waist." In other words, when you see Jesus, the character traits of righteousness and faithfulness stand out as clearly as a belt or sash. When the elderly apostle John was given a vision of the end of time, he reported how the Messiah will appear in his glory: "I saw heaven standing open and there before me was a white horse, whose rider is called Faithful and True" (Rev. 19:11). At the culmination of history, Jesus could choose from among dozens of titles to describe himself. At that critical moment, Jesus chooses to be called Faithful and True. We will begin the eternal celebration of his victory with a reminder that he has treated us faithfully.

Through His Shaping of Our Lives

The final vehicle God uses to reveal his faithfulness may not be the most dramatic, but it is certainly the most personal. He demonstrates his faithfulness in the way he shapes our lives.

This is where the rubber of God's truth meets the road of our experience. So far, the evidence we've looked at for God's faithfulness has been rather objective. But his personal dealings with us are subjective; our daily experiences allow us to get an intimate, inside look at his faithfulness firsthand.

As we study God's faithfulness, it is easy to see it as an abstract quality revealed in creation, his people, his Spirit, his character, his Word, and his Son, Jesus. If we are not careful we think about God's faithfulness as something akin to "The Force" in a Star Wars movie; an invisible hand mysteriously and unexpectedly moving on our behalf and dependent upon our performance.

On the contrary, God's faithfulness is most profoundly experienced in our human weakness, sin, temptation, and failure. "The LORD is near to the brokenhearted and saves those who are crushed in spirit" (Ps. 34:18 NASB). Our tendency, unfortunately, is to run away from God when we fail, sin, or struggle with temptation.

I am going to ask you to let me put on my teacher's hat for just a few moments and be very specific about how God works in shaping our lives. At the end of this section of the book, I have a story to share that I think will help you experience God's faithfulness in a profoundly deep and personal way.

Here are four specific and recurring instances in our lives when God desires to reveal his faithfulness:

1. GOD DEMONSTRATES HIS FAITHFULNESS WHEN WE ARE WEAK.

No one admits this truth more clearly or unexpectedly than the apostle Paul. This spiritual powerhouse had one of the greatest minds in the first century, but he humbly admitted his weakness:

> To keep me from becoming conceited because of these surpassingly great revelations, there was given me a thorn in my flesh, a messenger of Satan, to torment me. Three times I pleaded with the Lord to take it away from me. But he said to me, "My grace is sufficient for you, for my power is made perfect in weakness." (2 Cor. 12:7–9)

Paul trained under the famous Jewish rabbi Gamaliel. By reputation, he was a Pharisee of the Pharisees, a prime example of righteousness and knowledge. He eventually wrote thirteen books in the New Testament. But this spiritual superhero had bad days. A weakness tormented him, and he cried out to God for relief. Calling it a "thorn" doesn't tell us what it was, but it does let us know that the pain and discomfort were continuous—just like the kind many of us have. But Paul knew what to do. He turned to God in prayer. And God answered his prayer: "Paul, get used to this. You are not going to be delivered *from* this thorn; you'll get delivered *through* this thorn."

In Paul's weakness, God proved his faithfulness. Those of us who avoid discomfort like the plague have a hard time accepting this aspect of God's dealings with us. Our reluctance doesn't faze him for a moment. There are bigger issues at stake than our comfort. God says to us what he said to Paul: "My grace— my unmerited loving presence, compassion, character, my Spirit's manifestation of the life of

257

the eternal God—my grace is sufficient for you for my power is made perfect in weakness. When the world sees that I sustain you in spite of your utter weakness, it will know that it's all about me instead of all about you."

Paul's response is amazing: "Therefore I will boast all the more gladly about my weaknesses, so that Christ's power may rest on me. That is why, for Christ's sake, I delight in weaknesses, in insults, in hardships, in persecutions, in difficulties. For when I am weak, then I am strong" (2 Cor. 12:9–10). What a remarkable way of handling life's inevitable problems! "I delight in—I thoroughly enjoy myself when I'm reminded of—my weakness, in insults, in hardships, in persecutions, and in difficulties."

Can you say that? We usually say, "I'm hanging in there, I'm trying to handle this, I'll keep a good attitude as long as I can, but you've got to understand." Paul wasn't a "barely making it" kind of guy. He was an overcomer in the face of the things that tend to overwhelm the rest of us. How can he say this? Here's his reason: "For when I am weak, then I am strong." He doesn't say, "For when I am weak I act like I'm strong." He's very clear on the source of weakness and the source of strength. The point of admitting weakness is not to wallow in defeat but to allow God's strength to be displayed in us.

When God lets difficult circumstances into your life involving health, relationships, money, jobs, or family, it's easy to get so desperate that you just throw your hands up and say, "O God, I can't take one more minute of this!" But if you come to him, he will manifest his power and grace. The rest of us will look at your life and ask, "There's no human explanation for this. How are you doing it?" We will know it isn't your ability—it's God in you, the hope of glory. It's God showing us that he is faithful.

2. God reveals his faithfulness when we're tempted.

There is a difference between temptation and sin. Being tempted means you are distracted and have desires. You recognize a lure to do something—to indulge in a lustful thought, to steal, to be critical, to gossip, or to indulge in any other aspect of our vast opportunities for disobedience. Temptation occurs when all the circumstances suddenly align into an attractive opportunity. The moment you are tempted, you're like a fish eyeing a lure. The item looks glittery and promising. Unspoken whispers say, "This will make you feel good, you deserve this, it will take care of your problems, it's just what you need." It's like being on a diet while you are shopping at Costco. You see a free sample of chocolate cake right in front of you, inviting you to try it. You may walk around it again and again, looking at it from every angle as you walk through the aisle—and if you do, you're daring temptation to get the best of you. But until you take a bite and add that cake to your cart, you're just being tempted.

One of the most common excuses for giving in to temptation is a sense of uniqueness—"I have a special weakness and I'm genetically predisposed when it comes to that sin," or, "No one's had to face my kind of temptation before." God's Word gives a disarming response: "No temptation has seized you except what is common to man. And God is faithful; he will not let you be tempted beyond what you can bear. But when you are tempted, he will also provide a way out so that you can stand up under it" (1 Cor. 10:13). One hundred percent of the time, you can overcome temptation—not because you're strong, but because God is faithful. There is a way out of every temptation every time, if you'll take it. Like everyone, you're going to be tempted millions of times in your life. At that point you can try to rely on your own strength, or you can depend on God to provide a "way out." His way is not a matter of your willpower. Be honest about your struggle and ask him to show you the escape route that he has provided, and he will. It's guaranteed. He will demonstrate his faithfulness by helping you "stand up under" any temptation that comes your way.

3. GOD LONGS TO SHOW HIS FAITHFULNESS TO US WHEN WE SIN.

Even when we have failed to take advantage of his way of escape from temptation, God doesn't give up on us. He shifts to the next opportunity to demonstrate faithfulness toward us. First John 1:9 gives us the specifics: "If we confess our sins, he is faithful and just and will forgive us our sins and purify us from all unrighteousness." Accepting our confession, God remains true to both his faithfulness and justice, and he forgives us.

You became a believer when you put your trust in Jesus, his work on the cross, and his resurrection. At a moment in time, you realized you needed a Savior, repented, changed your mind about sin and life, and turned to God. Christ came into your life and his Spirit took up residence in you. Now you have a new relationship with him.

But you find something amazing in this new relationship—you still sin. The battle rages, flesh against spirit. Believe it or not, God is not surprised. He included an "in-case-of-failure" component in your relationship with him. When you realize you have sinned, you stop, come to him, confess that what you did was wrong, and accept the consequences and his forgiveness. He is faithful.

For many of us, this process is familiar, but we tend to think it only applies to "little sins." We're quick to ask God for forgiveness for a glance at pornography, a harsh word, or a lustful thought, but I know Christians who are trapped in affairs, captive to cyber-porn, or deeply mired in deception. They believe they are beyond the reach of God's faithfulness. People carry terrible secrets, painful wounds, and deal with nightmares for years, partly because they believe God refuses to handle such filth.

Perhaps you've had thoughts like these: "I know God forgives me, but I just can't forgive myself," or "I can't see how God can ever forgive me for what I did. I knew better. I feel such shame, I feel so bad, I feel so dirty, and I feel so sinful." If those quotes reflect your feelings, here's an important theological lesson that can set you free: *The issue of your past sin and forgiveness has nothing to do with you being able to forgive yourself!* If you agree with God about your sin, he is faithful and just to forgive you (1 John 1:9). When Jesus died on the cross, a transaction occurred. He covered your sin once and for all. The issue is whether you will accept that God's solution for sin is true in your case. If God is faithful and just, then Christ's blood atoned for your sin, and forgiveness is available to you. It's really not about you forgiving you; it's about you accepting what God has done. Not to do so underestimates the blood that Christ shed for you. When Christians claim that Christ forgave their sin in general but can't forgive their specific sins, they are saying that his work on the cross wasn't quite good enough.

If the Scripture says God has faithfully removed our sins as far as the east is from the west (Ps. 103:12), why are we trying to drag them back home? We can be free and clean by asking the Spirit of God to give us a sense of what's already occurred in our lives. We don't need to forgive ourselves. We need to trust what has already happened.

God is faithful, and he wants to show you that he is not just faithful when you're a good boy or a good girl. He's faithful all the time because that's who he is, and that is how he longs for you to see him.

4. GOD WANTS TO SHOW US HIS FAITHFULNESS EVEN WHEN WE UTTERLY FAIL.

When it comes to our relationship with God, it's impossible to overestimate the importance of one person in the relationship being absolutely faithful. One of the Bible's favorite adjectives about God's attributes is "unfailing," as in unfailing kindness and unfailing love. By contrast, one of our most consistent traits as humans is failure. Every time we fall short in measuring up to God's standard, his faithfulness offers to make up the difference. In Paul's last letter to Timothy, he highlighted the challenge to "be strong in the grace that is in Christ Jesus" (2 Tim. 2:1 NASB). In other words, depend strongly on God to do what you cannot do for yourself. In order to illustrate the way God handles our relationships with him, the apostle describes four scenarios in 2 Timothy 2:11–13:

> It is a trustworthy statement:
>> For if we died with Him, we will also live with Him;
>> If we endure, we will also reign with Him;
>> If we deny Him, He also will deny us;
>> If we are faithless, He remains faithful, for He cannot deny
>>> Himself. (NASB)

The symmetry of the first three scenarios creates a rhythm: died/live; endure/reign; disown him/disown us. We almost have to read the fourth exchange twice because the previous ones lead us to expect a different response than Paul wrote: our faithlessness is met with God's faithfulness. The listed consequence in each of the previous scenarios all have the same thing in common with the last—God is faithful in every one. If we died with him, we can count on his faithfulness to let us live with him. If we endure, he will faithfully share his reign with us. If we deny him, he will deny us. In this contrast, Paul is talking about blessing, not talking about salvation. He makes the same point in 1 Corinthians 3:12–15, where he assures believers of their salvation, yet makes clear the consequences of their wood, hay, and stubble (denying him)—the actions and motives that were contrary to him. But then comes the entirely unexpected: in spite of our faithlessness, God remains faithful because that's who he is.

I distinctly remember when Christ was beginning to draw me to himself, and when I accepted his offer of salvation. At first, I felt euphoria and relief that God had taken care of my sins. But about two years into the Christian life, the bottom began to fall out. I got so frustrated with sinning all the time and struggling with junk that I finally said, "If I can't live this life consistently, I'm going to quit."

So I quit. I took my Bible and my "To God be the Glory" poster and shoved them in the bottom drawer of my dresser. I announced to no one in particular, "I'm done. I quit the Christian life. I'm out."

> **Paul makes the same point in 1 Corinthians 3:12–15, where he assures believers of their salvation, yet makes clear the consequences of their wood, hay, and stubble (denying him)—the actions and motives that were contrary to him.**

Even though I had opted out, I couldn't stop thinking about God. He wouldn't go away. I didn't read my Bible for days, but he continued to convict me of sin and bring parts of his Word to mind. He brought person after person into my life to encourage me. And I kept having positive thoughts about his love.

"You don't understand," I told him. "I took myself out of the game. I've turned in the uniform. I can't handle this kind of life."

And God responded in ways that reminded me of the passage in 2 Timothy. "You know, Chip, on my team, the reality of our relationship is unilateral. If you died with me and you understand that, then you're going to live with me and you'll experience me. If you endure hardship, there's a reward—you're going to reign with me. And if you deny me and decide not to live the life, then I'm going to deny you. You'll experience the discipline of my love and the consequences of your actions, and you'll miss the blessings of a righteous life.

"But Chip, if you just say, 'Hey, I'm out of here,' guess what—we made a deal. Even when you don't keep your part, I'll always keep mine. I'm God, and I change not."

He had me. I couldn't beat him, so I had to join him. In hindsight, I'm grateful for his persistence. Over time, I began to realize that God had allowed my crisis of faith for his faithful purposes. He didn't want me to remain passively committed, so he let me get miserable to the point of quitting. Then he confronted me with the painful truth—I could let go of him, but he was not going to let go of me. I decided I might as well get on the right side of the team and walk with him.

All of which brings us to the need for a response. If he is unilaterally faithful, we may wonder what our role in the relationship is. For example, if we already know that God is going to remain faithful, then how do we avoid careless faithlessness? And how do we deal with those times when we are faithless?

How Do We Respond to God's Faithfulness?

No matter how shocked we are over our own faithlessness, it never takes God by surprise or causes him to divert his purposes in our lives.

He longs for us to know at the deepest level of our hearts that he is faithful. He wants us to see that he really loves us, not because of who we are but because of who he is!

Now, are there consequences for living a life that's disobedient? Of course! But God faithfully uses everything—even those hard consequences—to lovingly, gently draw us back. He simply will not give up on us. He wants us to know that when we blow it, he's faithful. When we are weak, he will be faithful. Even when we deny him, he remains faithful.

Remember Peter, who managed to blow it completely all in one night? He made rash statements, acted impulsively, ran under pressure, and denied knowing Jesus. As much as we want to think we are not like Peter, he's a good example of how badly we often blow it. That's why he's also a good example of how God handles us. Peter was so ashamed that he quit and went back to fishing. He wasn't trying to find Jesus to make things right; Jesus went looking for him. Jesus helped him unpack his guilt and set him free. And that's exactly the way he is with us. He pursues us after our failures and leads us to restoration.

God's Word provides us with instructions for how to respond when we discover faithlessness in our lives.

1. Put your past behind you today.

If there's a skeleton in your closet, if you have sin in your life, or if you're not a believer, confess your sin. Claim the truth in 1 John 1:9: "If we confess our sins, he is faithful and just and will forgive us our sins and purify us from all unrighteousness." Agree with God about your sin and accept his remedy. Say to him, "I've blown it. Yes, I had an affair; yes, I am a workaholic; yes, I've made idols of my children; yes, I'm consumed with myself and my appearance; yes, I'm hooked on porn; yes, I abused that child; or yes, I had an unbiblical divorce. Yes, yes, yes, Lord. I blew it."

But don't stop there. God's purpose for repentance isn't to get you to beat yourself up with guilt and confession, but to move on to freedom. Pray, "I also acknowledge that what I've just confessed are the very reasons Jesus had to die on the cross for me. Jesus, I accept your shed blood, once and for all, wiping my slate clean. Thank you, Lord!"

Put your past behind you. God has taken care of it. The only one holding on to the past is you. In Christ, God no longer remembers your sin.

2. Bring your present problems, pain, and failures to Jesus today.

Paul did just that in 2 Corinthians 12 when he turned to God with his troubling weakness. He brought his problem in an attitude of complete trust. His response to God's answer demonstrated his trust. It turned Paul's hardship into an honor.

In Matthew 11:28–30, Jesus invites you today to let him comfort you. "Come to me, all you who are weary and burdened, and I will give you rest. Take my yoke upon you and learn from me, for I am gentle and humble in heart, and you will find rest for your souls. For my yoke is easy and my burden is light." Is this the kind of God you are worshiping? If you're worshiping a different kind of god, stop and take another look. God is the kind of God who, when you're tired, distant, and burdened with guilt, gives this invitation: "Just come to me and I'll give you rest."

He also says, "Take my yoke upon you." The words create a picture of two oxen sharing a yoke, which isn't a bad situation if one of the pullers is God Almighty. When you feel like you've blown it as a Christian,

Jesus says: "Why don't you team up with me and learn from me. I'm gentle and humble. I'm not going to come down on you. You'll find rest for your soul. Why don't you get out of the rat race and quit trying to live this life on your own?"

This is powerful imagery in an agricultural society, but it often doesn't translate well in an urban-centered culture. People wonder what God means by a yoke, and they aren't sure where the "rest" is.

One morning I was tired to the bone. Even sleep didn't offer relief. I closed my eyes and began to pray my version of Peter's "Help me, Lord, I'm sinking!" prayer. "Lord, help me," I began. "Help me fight and help me pray, help me to be thankful, to trust in you, and to get my focus off myself, my problems, my demands, and my pressures. Help me focus on who you are and how faithful, strong, powerful, willing, and loving you are to fulfill your highest and best purposes in and through my life." As long as I was talking to God, the darkness seemed to roll back. But as soon as I took a breath, the tide came rushing in and I felt suffocated. "O Father," I cried, "I can't remember feeling this low for this long. I'm discouraged over small things, I'm doubting my decisions, and I'm tired. Please give me your perspective and renew me. Please show yourself faithful, kind, and merciful."

My prayer wasn't fancy or pretty. It was ugly and desperate—as honest as I could be. That's the way God likes it. That's how we need to come. Impressive prayers only impress other people. God wants to hear your heart speak. He understands the confusion that you can hardly put into words.

For me, writing it down gets it clean and clear. I often record my prayers in my journal because that keeps my mind from wandering and keeps my soul on track. That's particularly important when I start making requests of God and voicing my commitment to him.

That morning I wrote, "Please forgive me, Mighty God, for not trusting you. Forgive me for my short fuse and my focus on myself instead of the needs of others. Forgive me for inwardly whining and outwardly complaining, and failing to be thankful when your blessings abound everywhere. Forgive me for the shallowness of my prayers, and my lack of concentration and mental discipline when I pray. Please give me a desire to trust and enjoy you and others rather than simply wanting to get bad stuff off my plate and focus on good stuff. Father, I want to entrust to you everything that is weighing me down. I come right now to cast all my anxieties on you, because I believe you care for me."

I wrote them down: my moods, my struggles, my inner condemnation, and my self-focus. I then gave the list to God and said, "I accept your forgiveness and cleansing right now."

Then I was amazed at how my mind began to fill with the faces and needs of other people in my life. I was able to entrust Theresa to God for safekeeping in a particularly difficult time she was facing. As my attention shifted to the needs of others, my sense of God's faithfulness began to push back the darkness in my life. I filled several pages with prayers and praise for what God was doing for me and others, evidences of his overwhelming faithfulness. By the time I closed my journal, I was out of the depths I had been in. None of my circumstances had changed, but just coming, owning my issues, and confessing my sin opened my eyes to God's gentle, humble love. I am convinced you will find God's faithfulness equally available to you.

3. Place your hope for the future in the One who will never let you down.

We began this chapter with a glimpse into the dismal conditions that surrounded Jeremiah's life and his feelings of despair. The old prophet brought his problems, pain, and failures to God and laid them bare, in all their bitterness and anger. But, the higher he piled all his complaints on the table, the more apparent it became to him that no matter how dark or bad his circumstances, they did not match God's faithfulness.

> Yet this I call to mind
> > and therefore I have hope:
>
> Because of the LORD's great love we are not consumed,
> > for his compassions never fail.
> They are new every morning;
> > great is your faithfulness.
> I say to myself, "The LORD is my portion;
> > therefore I will wait for him." (Lam. 3:21–24)

We taste God's faithfulness when we begin to trust him with our tomorrows and then watch to see what he does. Every morning presents us with an opportunity to experience a brand-new creation, beyond the unique design of the day itself, unlike any other in history. Jeremiah learned to greet each day with an assurance that the Lord was his "portion"—that God is the one solid, unmovable, reliable part of any day. No one else delivers like he does. We must learn to place our hope in Christ—not in stuff, not in good health, not in the future, not in the stock market, not in the ups and downs of dating life or marriage.

Every other basis for hope will let us down. Only in Christ do we find the secret to a life of unending joy and peace, because he is the only one who will "come through for us" 100 percent of the time in any and every situation forever. The more we allow God to do what he longs to do—show himself faithful and powerful in our lives—the more we will be inclined to respond to him.

4. Tell someone each day how God has been faithful to you.

We can verbally respond to God's faithfulness two ways: we can tell him what we think of his compassionate consistency toward us, and we can tell others about what he has done for us. The Psalms are filled with examples we can use to train ourselves in both forms of response; the psalmists were constantly telling God how much they appreciated his faithfulness and inviting others to recognize his attributes. Jeremiah recognized that there are new things to notice about God's faithfulness every morning, so if we decide we're going to make a daily practice out of telling someone else about God's character, we'll never run out of things to say.

Here are some of my favorite examples in the Psalms:

> But I will keep on hoping for you to help me;
>> I will praise you more and more.
> I will tell everyone about your righteousness.
>> All day long I will proclaim your saving power,
>> for I am overwhelmed by how much you have done for me.
> I will praise your mighty deeds, O Sovereign LORD.
>> I will tell everyone that you alone are just and good. (Ps.
>>> 71:14–16 NLT)

> I will sing of the LORD's great love forever;
>> with my mouth I will make your faithfulness known through
>> all generations.
> I will declare that your love stands firm forever,
>> that you established your faithfulness in heaven itself. (Ps.
>>> 89:1–2)

> Sing a new song to the LORD!
>> Let the whole earth sing to the LORD!
> Sing to the LORD; bless his name.
>> Each day proclaim the good news that he saves.

Publish his glorious deeds among the nations.
> Tell everyone about the amazing things he does. (Ps. 96:1–3
> NLT)

Every day, tell someone how God came through and that you've seen his faithfulness. Give people in your life permission to ask you frequently about God's faithfulness. Practice will improve your ability to spot examples. Remember that there will always be events around you that tempt you to doubt. Recognize that these temporary circumstances may claim your attention and your emotions, just like the terrible setting that faced Jeremiah that we looked at in the opening of this chapter. Like Jeremiah, don't hesitate to tell God what you see, but make sure to allow God's faithfulness to have the last word. When all is said and done, you will still have good reasons to sing with the old hymn writer: "Great is thy faithfulness, Lord, unto me."

My Experience with the Faithfulness of God

Someone has rightly observed that our children are the source of our greatest joys and greatest sorrows. This has certainly been the case for Theresa and me. We have four grown children married to wonderful spouses who have given us eleven amazing (I am very biased) grandchildren. Our big family photo of all twenty of us that hangs on the wall as you enter our home might reinforce the age-old stereotype many might have of a pastor's family—a happy, well-adjusted, blessed-in-every-way family with no problems.

In reality, the photo is the most powerful picture in my life of God's great faithfulness to his Word, his specific promises, and to two broken people from dysfunctional families shaped by alcohol and WWII–wounded fathers.

Theresa and I both came to Christ as adults. Neither of us had ever read the Bible, but God brought faithful people into our lives to disciple us. We married and prepared for ministry only to discover we did not know how to communicate, resolve conflict, or how to deal with the baggage of our pasts. God used a professor and faithful marriage counselor in our lives to teach us how to love, forgive, and heal.

Prior to coming to Christ, Theresa was abandoned by her first husband. She was left to raise twin baby boys alone, while he left town with another woman. What I did not understand is how much power that abandonment had over her view of herself. I saw her as a beautiful, amazing woman of God, but she saw herself in a negative light and seemed to continually battle fears of rejection and abandonment. God in his faithfulness showed me how his love could heal a heart and transform a life.

My overachieving, workaholic, performance orientation was great for getting As in school and an athletic scholarship to college, but the twin boys I was privileged to adopt as my own had to endure an over-the-top dad who was far too hard on them and had no clue what he was doing. But God in his great faithfulness brought father figures into my life and moved me to study the Scriptures on what it meant to be a father.

Perhaps our greatest heartache was when one of our boys went through a season of rebellion. It was the longest and most painful four years of our lives. My parenting style and lack of wisdom did nothing but throw gasoline on the fire of his journey away from Christ, but God in his great faithfulness fulfilled the promise that Theresa held on to in her despair as a single mother—"that all [her children] will be taught by the LORD" (Isa. 54:13).

My prayer was simply that God would restore my son to himself, but God in his great faithfulness turned his heart fully to Jesus and put songs within him that the nations would sing in praise and glory to his name.

When I was younger I dreamed of having three sons and a daughter who would grow up, marry well, and walk strongly with the Lord. I longed to be a great example, to work hard and to do it "right," whatever that meant. Yet now as I look back, I see it was our brokenness, struggles, insecurities, and fears that drove us to God's Word, inspired us to claim his promises, and caused us to pray and seek him in our desperation.

In a word—our family and our family picture are nothing more but nothing less than a picture of God's great faithfulness!

Live It Out—B.I.O.

"Bio" is a word that is synonymous with "life." Found in those three simple letters, B.I.O. is the key to helping you become the person God wants you to be.

B *Come BEFORE God daily.* Meet with him personally through his Word and prayer to enjoy his presence, receive his direction, and follow his will.

I *Do Life IN COMMUNITY weekly.* Structure your week to personally connect in safe relationships that provide love, support, transparency, challenge, and accountability.

O *ON MISSION 24/7.* Cultivate a mindset to "live out" Jesus's love for others through acts of sacrifice and service at home, work, play, and church.

Come BEFORE God

• Write the following definition on a notecard, smartphone, or tablet and place it where you will read it when you get up in the morning and when you go to bed. Don't try to memorize it. Simply read it in a spirit of prayer and let the reality of God's faithfulness pour over your soul.

> Upon God's faithfulness rests our whole hope of future blessedness. . . . Only as we have complete assurance that He is faithful, may we live in peace and look forward with assurance to the life to come.[2]
>
> A. W. Tozer

And so today, I choose to place my hope in you, Lord Jesus; because you have promised to "come through for me" 100 percent of the time in any and every situation forever.

• Near the definition, write Lamentations 3:21–24 and meditate on that thought. Each time you read it, begin by asking, "What would it be like if I really believed that God's faithfulness never ends? How would that change how I see myself and how I relate to others?"

> This I call to mind
>   and therefore I have hope:
> Because of the LORD's great love we are not consumed,
>   for his compassions never fail.
> They are new every morning;
>   great is your faithfulness.
> I say to myself, "The LORD is my portion;
>   therefore I will wait for him." (Lam. 3:21–24)

• Join me in making the following prayer your own for the next seven days:

O Lord, my faithful, unfailing God, as I consider your faithfulness and remember its newness each and every morning, grant that I might

- *put all my sin behind me, covered by your faithfulness to forgive,*

- *bring every detail of every problem to you,*

- *abandon all false hopes and place all my hope in you, and*

- *be zealous to tell of your faithfulness.*

Let the certainty of your faithfulness sink into my heart. Help me always to trust that you will come through 100 percent of the time in every situation, now and forever. In Jesus's name, Amen.

- In what ways has God personally shown you his faithfulness, even in moments of your weakness?

- Reflect on the lyrics of the worship song "Forever Reign," written by Jason Ingram and Reuben Morgan. You may even want to sing this song as a personal prayer to God.

Do Life IN Community

- How has God shown his faithfulness to you in the shaping of your life?

- Over forty times in the Bible, God tells his people to "remember." It is easy to forget God's faithfulness to us, especially during a difficult time. The Israelites would select stones as a sign to remember God's specific faithfulness to them (Josh. 4:1–7). Select a rock to help you remember one specific way God has shown his faithfulness to you. Place the rock in a location that you will see it and "remember."

• Share with someone how God has been faithful to you.

Be ON Mission

• In God's faithful shaping of your life, he has given you talents, resources, and experiences that you can use to invest in the lives of others. What might these be?

• Prayerfully consider how God might want you to use them.

11

HOW HAS YOUR VIEW OF GOD CHANGED?

Remember the vision test you took at the beginning of the book? Now that we have come to the end of this journey together, I want to encourage you to retake the test to see how your view of God has changed.[1]

Energy

Those who know God have great energy for God. When you have an accurate view of God, you have energy to get into his Word. When you see things that are wrong in the church, you have energy to lovingly fix them. When you see people in need, you have energy to move in for God, you have energy for prayer, and he becomes the priority in your life. If you have energy for God, you have a pretty accurate view of him. Where do you fit on the continuum today? Circle the number that represents you.

Low Energy / Vague Knowledge   High Energy / Clear Knowledge

0	1	2	3	4	5	6	7	8	9	10

Thoughts

Those who know God have great thoughts of God. When you know God, there will be times in your prayer when you will hear yourself talking about his majesty, his glory, his righteousness, his holiness, and his purity. You will sit in quiet silence, overwhelmed with his greatness. You will discover that it is possible to love God with your mind.

On the scale below, where do your thoughts about God fall? What comes to your mind when you bow your head and start to pray? Do you find your mind stimulated as you anticipate thinking about God? Circle the number that represents you.

Low Thoughts / Vague Knowledge   High Thoughts / Clear Knowledge

0	1	2	3	4	5	6	7	8	9	10

Boldness

Those who know God show great boldness for God. When you have an accurate view of God in a fallen world, you have to continually choose between what the world thinks and what God says. People who really know God are bold in their choices for God.

Among the early apostles, the greatest evidence of being filled with the Holy Spirit had nothing to do with gifts, but rather with boldness. Hebrews 11 is filled with references to great women and men of faith, and the examples used to describe them almost always have something to do with their confidence in God. Knowing God, they went boldly.

If you are bold about your convictions and are not controlled by what other people think, you have an accurate view of God. Fear of exposure indicates low knowledge of God. Circle the number that represents you.

Low Boldness / Vague Knowledge						High Boldness / Clear Knowledge				
0	1	2	3	4	5	6	7	8	9	10

Contentment

Those who know God have great contentment in God. When you have an accurate view of God, you understand that he is all-knowing, all-seeing, all-powerful, and thoroughly good. He is *for* you. You can have difficulties, but you're not uptight and you're not anxious and you're not worrying because your life is under his care.

You say, "This tribulation is a struggle, but the King of the universe with all his resources, who gave his Son for me and dwells in me, will work this out. It may be hard and I may have some ups and downs, but I have a peace that surpasses understanding." Those who have great contentment in God reveal an accurate view of God. How does your present level of contentment measure up? Circle the number that represents you.

Low Contentment / Vague Knowledge						High Contentment / Clear Knowledge				
0	1	2	3	4	5	6	7	8	9	10

I trust that you will experience great encouragement as you see clearly the progress that you have made as you have grown through knowing, seeing, and experiencing God. I encourage you to continue to use this vision test as a gauge to measure your view of God, knowing that our life in Christ is an ongoing journey.

CONCLUSION

She made her way down the back streets and alleyways, carefully peering around corners before she turned them, making sure no one was around. At noon, even the narrowest passages offered no relief from the sun, but she didn't mind. Shade was a luxury for others, and it kept them inside during her daily, discreet visit to the well. It was the only way to avoid their stinging whispers.

The large jug dug into her shoulder, and it would dig even deeper on the trip home when it was full of water. Even so, it was the least of her burdens. There was nothing heavier than having to make this trip through the morning crowds. She would gladly carry the weight alone if doing so would avoid the condemnation she felt from their stares. A heavy load of water was nothing compared to the shame.

To her dismay, a man was at the well—a Jew, from the looks of him. She set her empty jug on the ground and pulled her head cloth closer around her face. She didn't think the stranger knew her but saw no sense in taking chances. Besides, if he were respectable, he'd never even acknowledge her presence. She could fill her pot quickly and head back home in peace.

But he spoke. Shocked by the sound of his words, it took her a minute to realize what he said. "May I have a drink?" he asked again. She glanced over her shoulder to make sure he wasn't speaking to someone approaching behind her. No, no one was there. Just her and, by the sound of the accent, a Galilean.

But there was no hint of contempt in his voice. That was unusual—and a good sign that the stranger had no idea who she was. Still, for a man to speak publicly to a woman and with such dignity! And for a Jew to speak to a Samaritan at all! Her curiosity got the best of her.

"You're a Jew and I'm a Samaritan," she said bluntly. "Why exactly are you asking me for a drink?"

He smiled and paused. She braced for a rebuke—or at least a pointed answer to her question.

"If you really knew who I was, you would have asked me for a drink. And I would have given you *living* water."

That wasn't an answer at all, but it did make her more curious. Here was a lone Jew, tired and helpless, without even a jug to hold water. Maybe he was teasing her. She decided to play along. "What would you draw it with? Where would you get this living water? Besides," she said proudly, "this is Jacob's well. It doesn't get any better than this."

"Everyone who drinks this water will get thirsty again," the Jew said cryptically. "But I have water that quenches thirst forever and even springs up into a well of its own—a well of eternal life."

She had never heard such intriguing words and such extravagant claims. The awkwardness of the conversation was forgotten. If she could have what this man offered, she would be happy. That was certainly worth the scorn of getting caught at the well with a Jewish man. So she asked for some of that water.

Again, he redirected her. "Go get your husband." Was that ancient protocol for a water-cooler discussion? It would have made the conversation more socially acceptable in most cases. But her case was different. She had several husbands—or none, depending on how one looked at it.

"I don't have a husband," she decided to answer. That would be the easiest way out of the predicament. Then maybe this stranger could get on with the living water he claimed to have.

"You're right," he said. No condemnation, no guilt trip. Just the truth. "You've had five, and the man you're with now is not your husband."

How embarrassing! How could he have known that? He saw right into her soul. She had gone to great pains to get to the well without being noticed, and now a complete stranger could apparently expose everything about her. Was this a divine setup to shame her? No, there was no hint of accusation in his voice. He must have been a prophet, a real authority from God. And surely prophets have more important issues to deal with. Maybe she could get his eyes off of her shortcomings and onto a bigger problem: the rivalry between Samaritans and Jews.

"Samaritans worship on Mount Gerizim, and Jews worship on Mount Zion. One of us is right, and one of us is wrong. Which one is it?"

Apparently, the answer was not that simple. This Jew affirmed Jewish worship, but not in its present form. Worship isn't about mountains, he told her. It's about what's in the heart, and more than that, it's about God.

Deep down, that interested her. Like everyone, she longed to know her Creator. And the prophet's refusal to be sidetracked made it clear: her Creator longed for the very same thing.

Jesus told her:

> Believe me, the time is coming when it will no longer matter whether you worship the Father here or in Jerusalem. You Samaritans know so little about the one you worship, while we Jews know all about him, for salvation comes through the Jews. But the time is coming and is already here when true worshipers will worship the Father in spirit and in truth. The Father is looking for anyone who will worship him that way. For God is Spirit, so those who worship him must worship in spirit and in truth. (John 4:21–24 NLT)

Jesus used the word "worship" or "worshiper" seven times in his conversation with the Samaritan woman. He made it clear that worship isn't about place. It doesn't happen simply because we know the right things about God. Rather, worship flows from spirit and truth—from knowing God himself.

In those moments by the well, Jesus radically altered a woman's view of God. She began to think of him in wider, deeper, and truer terms. She also began to think of herself in different terms. She started the conversation as a shamed sinner desperately avoiding the reality of her sin, and she ended up a joyful worshiper eager to tell everyone about someone worth meeting. Her encounter with Jesus transformed her into a persuasive witness. She began to know and worship God in spirit and in truth.

We started this journey into God's attributes by making the point that the way we think about God is ultimately the most significant aspect of our lives. Jesus opened the eyes of the Samaritan woman to realize that there was so much more to knowing God than her local tradition had taught her. He gave her an answer for the deep longing in her own soul.

He also gave her a glimpse of God himself. Jesus, the exact representation of God (Heb. 1:3) and the embodiment of the fullness of God

(Col. 1:19), showed God's character to someone who just went out to get some water. He was good to her, genuinely concerned for her welfare. He was sovereign, knowing the details of her past and aware of the divine appointment that led to their conversation. He was holy, confronting her sinfulness. He was wise, demonstrating the ability to draw her in without rejecting her as everyone else had done. He was just, not letting the judgments of men affect his mercy for this sinner, and dealing with her honestly and fairly from an eternal perspective. He was loving, patiently answering her questions and seeking her salvation above all else. And he was faithful, carrying out his will for an entire community through the witness of one redeemed sinner.

This story is one of many in which Jesus powerfully reflects the attributes of God. If you ever questioned whether God wants for you to see him, Jesus is the clearest answer. Not only has God spoken to us through his Word; the Word became flesh and dwelt among us. What greater evidence could we ask for? That would never have happened if God were casual about our knowing him. God clothed himself in humanity in order to demonstrate exactly who he is. He wants us to see him—and to see him as he really is.

The chapters you have just read have been prayerfully written to help you sense that. I hope they have done more than increase your factual knowledge about God. You may be able to recite the seven attributes I chose to highlight, and that's a great start. But I don't want you to stop until you have experienced those attributes in their breathtaking glory. I pray you will eagerly seek to let your knowledge make that eighteen-inch journey from your head to your heart, so that you can intimately, personally, and deeply know the God who loves you as only your Creator can. I trust you have been filled with a longing to worship the Father in spirit and truth. As you have turned these pages and lingered around the well of God's attributes, hoping to satisfy your thirst for deeper understanding, I pray that God has approached you unexpectedly and offered you repeated drinks from his soul-quenching spring. If you know Christ as Savior and Lord, that spring is actually welling up inside of you. Through him, you are becoming more intimately aware of the God who longs for you to see him.

APPENDIX

How to Have a Personal Relationship with God

The place to start a personal relationship with God is the same place where any relationship starts—with an introduction.

First, you need to know that God, in Christ, has already done something for you that you could never do for yourself. That's the good news. In order to understand why this is good news, you have to hear the bad news. You see, the Bible clearly teaches that we've all sinned and fallen short of the glory of God (Rom. 3:23). Your sin and my sin separate us from a holy God. Sin is a debt that keeps getting larger, and we have no way to make a payment. We are spiritually bankrupt.

Unless we get outside help, the consequences of our spiritual bankruptcy are predictable—punishment, death, and eternal separation from God. The first half of Romans 6:23 describes these results succinctly: "For the wages of sin is death." Fortunately, the good news comes in the second half of that verse. Outside help is available, and it's absolutely free. "For the wages of sin is death, but the gift of God is eternal life in Christ Jesus our Lord."

You may wonder how eternal life can be a free gift to sinners. Well, it's free to us, but it cost someone a lot. The Bible teaches that when Jesus died on the cross, he paid for your sin and mine once and for all, in our place (see Rom. 5:8). He settled our account (see Col. 2:13–15). The death of Christ is God's gift of grace toward you.

Simply knowing what Christ has done does not place you in a relationship with him. Admitting your sin is the first step. Understanding the just consequences of your sin is the next step. Realizing that Christ has paid for your sin once and for all is the third step. But it doesn't stop there. You must personally receive God's gift by faith. The Scriptures declare, "Yet to all who received him, to those who believed in his name, he gave the right to become children of God" (John 1:12).

You must receive the gift, not simply know about it. If you have never received him, Jesus is saying to you at this moment, "Here I am! I stand at the door and knock. If anyone hears my voice and opens the door, I will come in and eat with him, and he with me" (Rev. 3:20).

This is the offer that the eternal God makes to you through Jesus Christ. He wants to be with you always. And he wants you to be with him always. Why? Because he loves you!

So the ball's in your court. What will you do with this marvelous and amazing offer of forgiveness of your sins and a relationship with God through Jesus Christ? Will you pray right now to receive him into your life? Will you admit your sin and turn from it?

You can come to God right now through Jesus Christ. You can, through a brief prayer, express the earnest desire of your heart to become a member of God's family. If you are willing, you might pray in this way:

Dear God, I admit today that I'm a sinner. I know that I've done many things wrong and hurt many people. I deserve to be punished for my sin, but I believe that Christ died to pay for my sin, if I would but receive his sacrifice as a gift. Right now I trust that Christ took my place in his death, and that by his resurrection, he guaranteed his offer of eternal life to me. I receive you into my life right now as my Savior. Help me to become the person that you want me to be. Help me to walk with you all the days of my life. Thank you, Almighty God, that from this day forward I will never be alone. Thank you for being with me always. Amen.

NOTES

Introduction

1. A. W. Tozer, *The Knowledge of the Holy* (New York: HarperCollins, 1961), 1.

Chapter 2 Seeing God with 20/20 Vision

1. Tozer, *Knowledge of the Holy*, 1.

2. Ibid.

3. Ibid.

Chapter 3 God Longs for You to See Him

1. The tool referred to here and included in chapter 11 follows closely the pattern outlined by J. I. Packer in his peerless book *Knowing God* (Downers Grove: InterVarsity, 1993).

Chapter 4 The Goodness of God

1. Tozer, *Knowledge of the Holy*, 82.

2. Packer, *Knowing God*, 162, emphasis in original.

3. Ibid.

4. Ibid.

5. Tozer, *Knowledge of the Holy*, 82–83.

6. Ibid.

Chapter 5 The Sovereignty of God

1. Tozer, *Knowledge of the Holy*, 108, emphasis added.

2. If you want to examine God's remarkable revelation through Christ more thoroughly, spend some time pondering these passages: on his birth—Galatians 4:4; Matthew 2:3–6; on his prophecy-fulfilling life—Matthew 4:14; 12:15–21; on his power over the natural order—Matthew 8:23–27; 9:1–26; 14:15–21; on his teaching—John 8:48–58; on his death and resurrection—John 10:17–18; on his ascension and reign—Acts 1:9–11; Revelation 19:11–21.

Chapter 6 The Holiness of God

1. Tozer, *Knowledge of the Holy*, 104.

2. "Porn Epidemic in Churches Prompts Christian Filmmakers to Rally Pastors," *Christian News Wire*, June 11, 2014, http://www.christiannewswire.com /news/3558374284.html.

3. "New Study Shows Trends in Tithing and Donating," Barna Group, April 14, 2008, https://www.barna.org/barna-update/congregations/41-new-study-shows-trends -in-tithing-and-donating#.Vz9Xo1c9bbE.

4. Tozer, *Knowledge of the Holy*, 104.

Chapter 7 The Wisdom of God

1. Tozer, *Knowledge of the Holy*, 63.

2. Ibid., 60.

3. Ibid., 60–61.

4. Packer, *Knowing God*, 91–92.

5. Dr. Charles Ryrie (class notes, Dallas Theological Seminary, Dallas, TX, 1982).

Chapter 8 The Justice of God

1. Tozer, *Knowledge of the Holy*, 87.

2. Packer, *Knowing God*, 142.

3. C. S. Lewis, *Mere Christianity* (New York: Macmillan, 1952), 7.

4. C. S. Lewis, *The Great Divorce* (New York: Macmillan, 1946), 72–73.

Chapter 9 The Love of God

1. Henri J. M. Nouwen, *Life of the Beloved: Spiritual Living in a Secular World* (New York: Crossroad, 1992), 27–28; quoted in Brennan Manning, *Abba's Child: The Cry of the Heart for Intimate Belonging* (Colorado Springs: NavPress, 1994).

2. Charles Ryrie, *Basic Theology* (Chicago: Moody, 1999), 44.

Chapter 10 The Faithfulness of God

1. Tozer, *Knowledge of the Holy*, 79.

2. Ibid., 81.

Chapter 11 How Has Your View of God Changed?

1. The tool included in this section follows closely the pattern outlined by J. I. Packer in his peerless book *Knowing God* (Downers Grove: InterVarsity, 1993).

Chip Ingram is the senior pastor of Venture Christian Church in Los Gatos, California, and teaching pastor and CEO of Living on the Edge, an international teaching and discipleship ministry. A pastor for over thirty years, Chip has a unique ability to communicate truth and challenge people to live out their faith. Chip is author of many books, including *The Real Heaven*; *The Invisible War*; and *Love, Sex, and Lasting Relationships*. Chip and his wife, Theresa, have four grown children and eleven grandchildren and live in California.

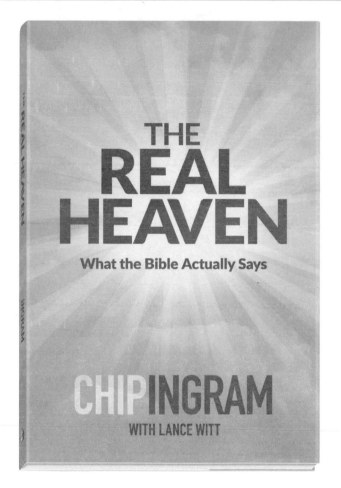

ALSO AVAILABLE

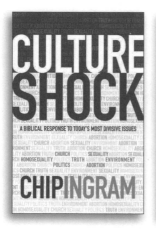

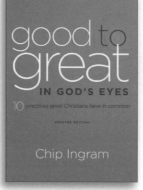

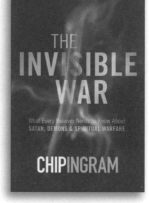

Chip Ingram shows you how to bring light rather than heat to the most controversial issues of our day. It's your must-have guidebook to replacing reactionary hate with revolutionary love.

"This book will redirect, empower, and inspire you on your own journey to greatness."

—**Gregg Dedrick**, former president, KFC

The Invisible War is a balanced and Biblically informed book that examines what every believer needs to know about Satan, demons, and spiritual warfare.

BakerBooks
a division of Baker Publishing Group
www.BakerBooks.com

FROM CHIP INGRAM

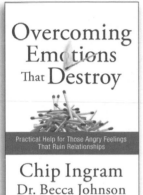

"I loved this book! From the searing first sentence, it delivers on its promise to lay bare the common failings of the human heart."

—**Gary Thomas**, author of *Sacred Marriage* and *Holy Available*

Whether single, single again, or wanting more from your marriage, you can begin the delightful journey toward a lasting, loving relationship. This practical, insightful book will show you how.

If you're fed up with our sex-saturated culture and are tired of being told to "just wait until you're married," then check out the Biblical understanding of sexuality.

THERE IS A DEEP SENSE OF UNEASE IN OUR RAPIDLY CHANGING WORLD. We all know something has been lost but don't know why or where it all leads. Popular culture says it's all about *me*—that the end justifies the means, that love means self-satisfaction, that status and appearance are what count. And this ultimately self-destructive perspective has thoroughly infiltrated the church as confusion replaces conviction.

OUR DISTORTED VIEW OF GOD IS AT THE ROOT OF ALL OF OUR PROBLEMS.

We've created a god in our minds who only faintly resembles the God of Scripture. These mental idols comfort our emotions, but they are powerless to deliver us from evil or transform our lives. The way back, the path of hope, starts with knowing God for who He really is.

When you join Chip Ingram in this in-depth study of seven attributes of God—His goodness, sovereignty, holiness, wisdom, justice, love, and faithfulness—you'll see Him in a whole new light. It will change the way you think about God, yourself, and others. You will pray and live with a deep peace and a renewed purpose as you see Him as He longs to be seen.

CHIP INGRAM is the senior pastor of Venture Christian Church in Los Gatos, California, and teaching pastor and CEO of Living on the Edge, an international teaching and discipleship ministry. A pastor for over thirty years, Chip has a unique ability to communicate truth and challenge people to live out their faith. Chip is the author of many books, *Culture Shock*, *The Real Heaven*, *The Invisible War*, and *Love, Sex, and Lasting Relationships*. Chip and his wife, Theresa, have four grown children and twelve grandchildren and live in California.

US $16.99   CLGN Christian Living
ISBN 978-0-8010-1889-3

51699

9 780801 018893

BakerBooks
a division of Baker Publishing Group

www.bakerbooks.com